John
Encountering
Christ in a
Life-Changing
Way

Bruce BICKEL
&
Stan JANTZ

HARVEST HOUSE™ PUBLISHERS

EUGENE, OREGON

Cover by Left Coast Design, Portland, Oregon

Cover photo by Steve Terrill, Portland, Oregon, www.terrillphoto.com

Harvest House Publishers, Inc. is the exclusive licensee of the trademark, CHRISTIANITY 101.

JOHN: ENCOUNTERING CHRIST IN A LIFE-CHANGING WAY
Copyright © 2003 by Bruce Bickel and Stan Jantz
Published by Harvest House Publishers
Eugene, Oregon 97402

Library of Congress Cataloging-in-Publication Data
Bickel, Bruce, 1952–
   John: encountering Christ in a life-changing way / Bruce Bickel and Stan Jantz.
      p. cm.—(Christianity 101™)
   ISBN 0-7369-0791-2 (pbk.)
   1. Bible. N.T. John—Commentaries. 2. Bible. N.T. John—Study and teaching. I. Jantz, Stan, 1952– II. Title. III. Series.
   BS2615.53 .B53 2003 226.5'07—dc21   2002010617

Printed in the United States of America

03 04 05 06 07 08 09 10 11 / DP-MS / 10 9 8 7 6 5 4 3 2 1

Contents

A Note from the Authors

*A*t the very start, we want to congratulate you. You are serious about studying the Bible, and we think that is great. Getting to know more about God is the best way to use your time, and studying the Bible is one of the best ways to learn what God wants you to know about Him.

After Reading John, You May Never Be the Same

Studying the Gospel of John is another shrewd move on your part. You are in good company. People like you have been interested in studying the Gospel of John for almost two thousand years. Many scholars consider the Gospel of John the best single book for learning all about Jesus Christ. We could hardly argue with that. But we think you're also likely to learn a lot about yourself by reading John. It gives you an insider's view to Jesus Christ. You'll see Him "up close and personal." And if you are like all of the other people who came face-to-face with Christ, your life will be changed.

Christianity 101 Bible Studies

Most people don't want to be Bible academicians. They don't desire to be fluent in the ancient Hebrew, Greek, and Aramaic languages. They just want a little help on understanding what the Bible means by what it says.

That's where this book comes in. We aren't intending to tell you everything that there is to know about the Gospel of John. That obviously couldn't happen in just 173 pages. We are just intending to give you a little extra help beyond what you can figure out on your own by reading the Bible. For example, we'll explain the historical and cultural setting—not all the time, but just when it will be particularly helpful to you. And we'll explain the meaning behind verses—not all the time, but just when a passage is particularly confusing to most people. The rest of the time, we'll back off and let the Holy Spirit give you divinely guided insight and meaning into what you are reading in God's Word.

This Bible study on John is part of a series called Christianity 101 Bible Studies. In this book (and the others in the series), we are trying to combine the best features of both a commentary and a Bible study:

- Like a commentary, this guide will give you the basics of what you need to know to get more meaning from what you read in the Bible. Occasionally we might slow the pace a bit to focus on the context of a particular word, but for the most part we'll assume that you want to get through a passage fairly quickly.

- Like a Bible study, we'll challenge you to do a little extra thinking about how to apply what the Bible says to your everyday life. At the end of each chapter we will pose several meaningful questions to help you draw out personal applications from the material. We aren't going to insult you by asking questions simply for the purpose of making sure you read the Bible passage. This means you won't be instructed to read John 11:35 (which reads, "Then Jesus wept"), and then be asked, "What did Jesus do?" We're going to get much more personal than that.

If you want more help in your study, look in the Dig Deeper section at the back of the book, where we have listed some resources that we think you'll find to be very helpful. And don't miss our online resource exclusively for users of the Christianity 101 Bible Studies at www.christianity101online.com. (More details are at the back of this book.)

Here's what you can expect to find in the pages that follow. In chapter 1, we'll tell you what sets the Gospel of John apart from the other Gospel accounts of Christ's life. In chapter 2, we'll give you some important background information about John (and why he was well-qualified to write a biography of Jesus) along with the major themes that run throughout the book. (If you are bucking for extra credit, you might want to do a quick speed-read through the book of John after reading chapter 2.) In chapters 3 through 13, we will progress through John, starting with the first verse and ending with the last one. We will tackle the book one passage at a time, pointing out meanings and messages that you will want to look for as you study these passages for yourself.

This Book Is for You If...

Maybe this is your first time using a resource for studying the Bible. Or maybe you are an experienced Bible student. Either way, perhaps you're wondering if this book will give you what you're looking for. We aren't exactly sure what you have in mind, but we think this book is for you if...

- Reading the Bible has always been a little confusing for you. It's like walking into a movie theater when the film is half over. You'd like some background information to better understand the context of what you are reading in the Bible.

- You enjoy reading the Bible, but you are interested in a little help to make the connection between Bible times and your life in the twenty-first century.

- You and a few friends are going to read the Gospel of John together. It's kind of a book club of the holy variety. Somehow you need to get the group focused on similar issues, but you want room for everyone to do some independent thinking.

And the Gospel of John Is Especially for You If...

Although there are 65 other books of the Bible to choose from, God may be directing you to the Gospel of John if...

- You are interested in finding out more about Jesus Christ. John is the biography of Jesus written by the person who was probably His closest friend on earth. If you are looking for a behind-the-scenes account of Christ's life, you'll find it in John.

• Your faith needs a boost. Your personal relationship with Jesus has been getting a little stale lately. You are anxious to recapture the enthusiasm that you used to have for Christ.

• You want to grow deeper in your commitment to Christ. You realize that Christianity is not so much a religion as it is a *relationship*...a relationship between you and Christ. And you can only develop that relationship by getting to know Him intimately. He already knows all about you, so now you've got some catching up to do.

One or More

We've designed this book so you can use it alone or in a group. Either way, you'll want to read the corresponding passages in the Bible. For personal study, we suggest reading the Bible text first, then reading the chapter in this book, and then going back and rereading the Bible passage again. For group study, you should read the Bible passage before and after your meeting. You'll be surprised how much more you draw out of the passage the second time after you have familiarized yourself with the contextual background.

The questions at the end of each chapter can be answered by you or discussed in a group. If you're going it alone, resist the temptation to simply read over the questions without actually answering them. If you are part of a group, make every attempt to answer the questions honestly and openly. Coming face-to-face with

Christ is always a humbling experience that demands self-examination.

Most important of all, remember that you've got a supernatural instructor to guide you through this study. The Holy Spirit is your personal teacher through this study, and He's better than any commentary:

> *But we know these things because God has revealed them to us by his Spirit, and his Spirit searches out everything and shows us even God's deep secrets* (1 Corinthians 2:10).

A Final Word Before You Begin

In Ephesians 5:2, we are told to follow the example of Christ. That's only possible when we learn who Christ is and what He did. That information is ready for you in the Gospel of John.

We're ready to give you a little help, but we want to stay in the background. We are convinced that you will sense God speaking directly to you as you study His Word, and we don't want to get in the way. Our prayer is that your study of the Gospel of John will change your life as you come to know Jesus better. It changed our lives.

Chapter 1

The purpose of this Gospel goes far beyond the mere creation of an opinion about its subject. The creation of a personal faith in Christ is the summit of its purpose; but this very faith has a still greater objective—*life*. The Gospel is intended to affect and transform the outlook and path of its reader. It is definitely planned with reference to his destiny.

—*Merrill C. Tenney*

What Is Going On?

Neither of us enjoys watching a rugby match. Actually, we've never watched one, but we're sure we wouldn't enjoy it. We've each seen glimpses on some obscure cable station as we surf the channels. The sport of rugby appears brutal, and that part intrigues us. It seems to have all of the body smashing of pro wrestling, except rugby is for real. But we don't know anything about the game of rugby. We don't know the rules or any of the strategy. To us, it just appears to be ugly brutes in short pants who bang their heads in a huddle or chase each other with a funny-looking football. We are sure we would enjoy the game if we knew what it was all about.

This first chapter is your "what it's all about" overview of the Gospel of John. We are going to give you some basics about the book and its author before you begin. We don't want you surfing past the Gospel of John as you read the Bible. You need to know that John wasn't just some ugly brute in a toga. We are sure that you'll enjoy the book when you know what it's all about.

A Different Perspective

*S*uppose you were interested in learning about Abraham Lincoln, but you were allowed to read only *one* of the many biographies about him. Which book would you select?

- a book written by a modern historian who knows about Lincoln only from books that other people have written

- a book written by a journalist who lived at the same time as Lincoln and actually saw Lincoln at public events

- a book written by one of the men who served in the Cabinet of Lincoln's presidential administration

- a book written by Lincoln's best friend, who was a close advisor to him from the time he was a struggling lawyer until his assassination

We guess that you'd pick the biography of Lincoln that was written by his best friend. You'd want to learn about Lincoln from the guy who knew him personally and knew him best. In the same way, the Gospel of John is the book for you if you want to know about Jesus Christ.

The Gospel of John gives you an up-close-and-personal encounter with Jesus Christ because it was written by the man who was probably Jesus' closest friend. John paints a picture of Jesus that goes far beyond just the facts of Christ's life. As he relates the stories of Jesus' life and explains their meaning and significance, you will see an intimate portrait of Jesus that you can find nowhere else.

A Biography That Stands Alone

The 66 books of the Bible include four biographies about Jesus. Together the first four books in the New Testament (Matthew, Mark, Luke, and John) are referred to as the Gospels. Having four separate profiles of Christ isn't overkill, and they don't overlap too much because each is written from a slightly different perspective.

> *Matthew:* This biography presents Jesus as the promised Messiah, the descendant of Abraham in the lineage of David, whose coming was predicted by the Old Testament prophets.

> *Mark:* This biography was written to Romans, who wouldn't have been interested in the Old Testament prophecies about the Messiah that were so precious to the Jews. The emphasis is on Christ's role as a servant.

Luke: Luke was a physician, so we should not be surprised that this biography emphasizes the humanity of Christ and His act of self-sacrifice for humanity.

John: The message is plain and simple: Jesus is the Son of God.

Yes, John is different from the other Gospels by reason of its predominant theme, but that isn't its only distinction.

---

*U*nderstanding the *D*ifferences *C*an *B*e a *R*eal *P*ane

The differences between the Gospels are often depicted on the stained glass windows in the cathedrals of Europe and the churches of North America. One favorite biblical text for these stained glass windows is Revelation 4:6-7, which mentions "four living beings" that many people apply to the four Gospel writers.

- *The Lion* represents Matthew's biography because it depicts Christ as the Messiah and the Lion of the tribe of Judah.

- *The Man* stands for Mark's Gospel because it is the simplest and most direct.

- *The Ox*, an animal used in sacrifices, depicts the book of Luke because it shows Christ as the universal sacrifice for humanity.

- *The Eagle* represents John's Gospel because of his soaring, heavenly description of Christ.

Three Against One

The Gospels of Matthew, Mark, and Luke are very similar to each other. So similar, in fact, that they are collectively referred to as the Synoptic Gospels because they can be read side by side for purposes of comparison. The events of Christ's life in the Synoptic Gospels track together in almost uniform sequence. But not so with the Gospel of John, which tells the account of Christ's life from an entirely different angle.

When John wrote his Gospel, he did some obvious editing work. He intentionally omitted certain facts and sayings of Jesus that are contained in the Synoptic Gospels. For example...

- When your family gathers at Christmastime for the traditional reading of the story of Christ's birth, you're reading from the Synoptic Gospels. That's because you won't find anything about the birth of Jesus in John. In fact, while the Synoptic writers cover the entire life span of Jesus, John covers only about five years of Christ's life preceding the Crucifixion and Resurrection.

- The Gospel of John also omits significant events in the life of Christ, such as His baptism, His temptation by Satan, the "communion" part of the Last Supper, and the Ascension.

- John also edited out of his Gospel the parable stories that Jesus told. These parables are some of the highlights of the Synoptic Gospels, but John doesn't mention a single one of them.

John wasn't a lazy author, and he didn't have a poor memory. He didn't include much of what is emphasized in the Synoptic Gospels because he was trying to emphasize a different aspect of Christ. And to get his point across, he included certain content that is exclusive to his Gospel.

- While the Synoptic Gospels often include short selections from Christ's conversations, John lays out the dialogue in much fuller detail. Christ's speech to the disciples and His prayer on the evening before His Crucifixion cover five chapters in John. Each of the Synoptic writers reduces this to part of one chapter. This is no small matter because the passage in John contains Christ's principal teaching about the Holy Spirit.

- John takes an expanded view of Jesus' public ministry. While the Synoptic Gospels start Jesus' public ministry at the point when John the Baptist is arrested, the Gospel of John covers a period where the activities of John the Baptist and Jesus overlap.

- Matthew, Mark, and Luke focus on Christ's ministry in Galilee and don't mention Jesus in Jerusalem until the last week of His life. John's Gospel, however, finds Christ in Jerusalem and Judea most of the time, with only an occasional trip into Galilee. This means that John covers certain events and encounters that aren't mentioned in the other Gospels, such as the interchange between Jesus and Nicodemus, the dialogue with the Samaritan woman at the well, and the raising of Lazarus.

The Publication Dates May Explain the Difference

The prevailing research pegs the writing of John sometime between A.D. 85 and 90. The other three Gospels had already been written by this time, with copies having been widely circulated within the Christian community for 30 years or more. John wasn't interested in providing a knockoff version of the biographies written by Matthew, Mark, and Luke. There was no reason to tell the same story in the same way.

Since the details of the life of Christ had already been widely publicized, John focused more on the *meaning* of the events than on the *description* of them. So, for example, while all four Gospels tell the story of Jesus miraculously feeding 5000 people, only John tells the after-dinner sermon that Jesus preached about being "the bread of life."

As you read through John, don't miss the spiritual explanation that often accompanies the telling of an event.

A General Audience

John's Gospel differs from the others for another reason. He wrote to a much broader audience than did the Synoptic writers. Each of them had a specific audience in mind:

- Matthew wrote to the Jews.

- Mark wrote to the Romans.

- Luke wrote to the Greeks.

But John wrote his Gospel to the world at large. After all, in the 30 or so years since the last Synoptic Gospel was written, Christianity had spread worldwide. No longer was it predominately limited to Jews in and around Jerusalem and Galilee who recognized Jesus as the Messiah. Through the missionary efforts of Paul and others, Christianity had worldwide appeal. Most Christians at the time of John's writing were Gentiles (non-Jews). Jerusalem had been destroyed in A.D. 70, and John was writing to a global audience that was geographically and generationally removed from Jewish culture and traditions. The truth of Christ was the same, but John needed to explain it in terms that the world could understand.

You might want to try reading through John as if you were someone who had no previous exposure to Jesus. Read as if this were your first introduction to Christ. With that mind-set, you are exactly the type of reader to whom John was writing. (This is precisely why the Gospel of John is a great starting place in the Bible for nonbelievers or new Christians.)

■ ■ ▣

$\mathcal{S}$tudy the $\mathcal{W}$ord

1. Suppose three people had already written a biography about your best friend. If you wanted to write a biography about that friend, what would you do to make your book different?

2. Look at these key thematic verses from each of the Gospels:

   Matthew 5:17

   Mark 10:45

   Luke 19:9-10

   John 20:30-31

   In what ways do these verses present different perspectives of Christ?

   In what ways are the messages of these verses similar?

3. Each of the four Gospels emphasizes that Jesus is the Son of God. Although none of them uses the term *incarnation* (the word that expresses the concept that God became a human being), this is a fundamental principle in John. Read Philippians 2:6-11 and Hebrews 2:14-15. What was God's purpose for becoming a man?

4. The four Gospels each present a different perspective of Christ. Which is your favorite approach? Why?

5. Before you go to the next chapter, tell what you know about John (the man). What do you think he was like?

Chapter 2

John has the most penetrating gaze of all the New Testament writers into the eternal mysteries and the eternal truths and the very mind of God. Many people find themselves closer to God and to Jesus Christ in John than in any other book in the world.

—*William Barclay*

From a Guy Who Knows

Maybe the reason that some history books seem dry and tedious is that the people who wrote them didn't live the events they wrote about. The emotion isn't in the writing because the authors weren't in the events.

You'll have no problem sensing the emotion of the episodes in the life of Christ as you read the Gospel of John. The Gospel's author, John, was right there by Christ's side as things happened. He was a witness to it all. But he wasn't a detached reporter who merely observed Christ for journalistic purposes. He was Christ's friend. And no one is better suited than John to describe how encountering Christ results in a changed life because John's own life was transformed in the process.

An Intimate Portrait

*T*alk is cheap. Anybody can spout off claims and promises. Are infomercials coming to mind? All too frequently we find that things, or people, don't live up to their hype. Whether it is the Wonder Mop or the NFL's first-round draft pick, actual performance often falls far below expectations.

Not so with Jesus Christ. The Gospel of John not only heralds Christ as a life changer but also offers evidence to prove He is. The best proof is the changed life of the Gospel's author, John. This makes sense. If God can change a life, a drastic change ought to be obvious in the life of the man who was closest to Christ.

The Beloved John

When you are reading the Gospel of John, you are getting a firsthand account of the life of Christ. That can't be said about the secondhand reports in the Gospels by Mark and Luke, who knew of Christ primarily through the testimony of others. And John's Gospel is even more intimate than the one written by his fellow disciple, Matthew. While they both traveled with Christ, Matthew wasn't part of the inner circle that Jesus established with John, Peter, and James. John, more than any other disciple, had a close bond with Christ. As you study the Gospel of John, watch for indications of their friendship in clues such as these:

- John was given preferred seating next to Christ at the Last Supper (John 13:23-25).

- Out of the 12 disciples, John was the only one who stayed with Jesus at the Crucifixion. And as He hung on the cross, Jesus asked John to attend to the care of His own mother (John 19:26-27).

- John never refers to himself by his name, but as "the disciple whom Jesus loved" (John 13:23).

John heard and saw more than any other disciple. When you read his Gospel, you get the intimate details and the dramatic messages of Christ that only a best friend would know.

Not Your Typical Author

When you look at the occupations of the men who wrote the biblical biographies of Christ, John seems least suited for the task of writing a Gospel. Matthew was a tax collector, so he knew how to handle paperwork. Mark was a missionary, so he had some religious training. Luke was a physician, so he was formally educated. But John was a fisherman.

If you have an image of a first-century fisherman in Galilee as being a rugged guy, you've got the right idea of John. If he were alive today, John would probably work on an oil rig off the coast of Greenland, and he might enter those Ultimate Warrior competitions on the weekend for fun. We aren't exaggerating. Jesus gave John and his brother, James, the nickname "Sons of Thunder." Thunder is explosive and unpredictable, and so was John. We know from the other Gospels that John was hot tempered and often on the verge of violently overreacting. That image of John doesn't come across in his own Gospel for several reasons:

- He was a senior citizen (somewhere between 80 and 90 years old) when he wrote his Gospel, so his blood pressure had probably subsided a bit.

- He was the elder statesman of Christianity when he wrote his Gospel. The other apostles had died as martyrs—he was the last survivor. Looking like a hothead wouldn't do his dignity much good (even if his offensive behavior was more than 50 years earlier).

But most significantly, John was a changed man from his early days as a novice disciple. His three-year friendship with Jesus changed him dramatically (but more about that a little bit later).

John was a younger cousin of Jesus. His mother, Salome, was the sister of Mary (the mother of Jesus). John and his brother, James, ran a very successful family fishing business with their father (Zebedee) in Capernaum on the shore of the Sea of Galilee. John was a follower of John the Baptist until Jesus called John to be one of His disciples.

After Christ's Crucifixion and Ascension, John became one of the leaders of the early Christian church in the city of Jerusalem (along with James and Peter). Tradition says that he later lived in Ephesus (probably after the destruction of Jerusalem in A.D. 70). Although he was not martyred for his faith, the Roman authorities exiled him on the island of Patmos. After he was released from exile, he returned to Ephesus where he apparently stayed until his death. While he lived in Ephesus, he wrote not only his Gospel but also the three letters *(epistles)* of 1 John, 2 John, and 3 John, as well as the book of Revelation (which recorded the end-times vision that he received from God while on Patmos).

An Eyewitness to the Whole Story

In his Gospel, John gets very specific about seemingly insignificant points in the life of Christ (which the Synoptic writers don't bother to mention). These are clues that he was an eyewitness to everything (and that he had a good memory). As you read through John's Gospel, look for his attention to detail:

- There were *six* water pots at the wedding feast in Cana (2:6).

- At the feeding of the 5000, the kid's lunch included *barley* loaves (6:9).

- The distance which the disciples rowed when Jesus walked to them on the water was *three or four miles* (6:19).

- There were *four* soldiers who gambled for Christ's robe as He hung on the cross (19:23).

As you read through John, remember that you are getting an insider's view that puts you right in the middle of the controversy that surrounded Christ.

It's All About Jesus Being the Son of God

John doesn't beat around a burning bush. He makes the purpose of his Gospel very clear. He wants everyone to know that Jesus is the Son of God and that eternal life comes only by believing on Him. He makes that point in undeniable terms by quoting the words of Christ in what may be the Bible's most famous verse:

For God so loved the world that he gave his only Son, so that everyone who believes in him will not perish but have eternal life (3:16).

Of course, the disciples had heard that statement at the time Jesus made it, but they didn't grasp it right away. So John sets out to establish through the words and actions of Jesus that He truly is the Son of God. And, just in case the readers of his Gospel were as dense as those first disciples were, he makes the point one final time near the end of the book:

Jesus' disciples saw him do many other miraculous signs besides the ones recorded in this book. But these are written so that you may believe that Jesus is the Messiah, the Son of God, and that by believing in him you will have life (20:30-31).

You'll notice that from the first verse to the last, John crafts his biography of Christ to emphasize Jesus as the loving Son of God who offers Himself as a sacrifice for our sins. He doesn't do this through skillful argumentation (as the apostle Paul does in his writing). Instead, John makes his point by selectively telling the things that Jesus said and did.

Look for the Metaphors of Christ's Identity as God

As you read through the Gospel of John, watch for Jesus' statements that identify Him as the Son of God, who provides a way of salvation for humanity. Christ often couched these statements in metaphors, and John weaves them throughout the Gospel so the theme of Christ as the Son of God is pervasive. Here are examples of the metaphors to look for:

- *I am the bread of life. No one who comes to me will ever be hungry again* (6:35).

- *I am the light of the world. If you follow me, you won't be stumbling through the darkness, because you will have the light that leads to life* (8:12).

- *I am the gate for the sheep...Those who come in through me will be saved* (10:7,9).

- *I am the good shepherd. The good shepherd lays down his life for the sheep* (10:11).

- *I am the vine; you are the branches. Those who remain in me, and I in them, will produce much fruit. For apart from me you can do nothing* (15:5).

Are you getting the idea of what to look for? We haven't given all of John's metaphors to you because we don't want to spoil your sense of adventure as you search his Gospel for the rest of them.

These examples are fairly evident, but some are less obvious, so you'll have to stay alert as you read the Gospel of John. For example, take notice when John the Baptist declares that Jesus is the "Lamb of God." The Jews had a daily ritual of sacrificing a lamb on the altar in the Temple. This was a sacred offering to God by the Jews in confession and acknowledgment of their sins. The Old Testament prophet Isaiah had compared the Messiah to a sacrificial lamb. Calling Jesus the "Lamb of God" was the same as saying that He was going to be the sacrificial offering for the people's sin.

Watch for Proof That Christ Had the Power of God

Of course, anyone can *say* they are God. But who can back it up with supernatural proof? To give credibility to the claims of Christ's lordship, John tells of several miracles performed by Jesus. He weaves them into the biography. As you read through John, watch for evidence of Christ's supernatural power in events such as these:

- changing water into wine (2:1-11)

- healing a lame man at the pool of Bethesda (5:1-9)

- feeding 5000 people from a bag lunch of five biscuits and two small fish (6:1-14)

- walking on the water (6:16-21)

- bringing Lazarus back to life after he had been dead and buried for three days (11:1-44)

John includes other miracles, so be watching for them. When you find them, you will notice something interesting. The Synoptic writers told of many more miracles by Christ, and each account seems to reveal Christ's compassion for humanity (by showing how He met people's physical needs). John knew of Christ's love and compassion, but he uses the miracles to show the divine power of Christ. See if you can pick up on that distinction as you read John's Gospel.

Don't Miss the Testimonials That Christ Is the Son of God

Remember that John was trying to make his readers deal with the issue of who Jesus was. If He was just a man, they could forget about Him. But if He was God, the readers would have to decide whether to accept Him or reject Him.

John's Gospel shows that some objective observers, when confronted with Christ, considered Him to be the Son of God. Watch for testimonials by these and other witnesses:

- John the Baptist: *So I testify that he is the Son of God* (1:34)

- Nathanael: *You are the Son of God* (1:49)

- Peter: *We know you are the Holy One of God* (6:69)

- Martha: *You are the Messiah, the Son of God* (11:27)

- Thomas: *My Lord and my God* (20:28)

A Close *E*ncounter of the *T*ransforming *K*ind

John wanted his readers to get to know Jesus. He knew their encounter with Christ, even though it wouldn't be face-to-face, would change their lives. That's exactly what had happened to him. After being mentored (spiritual word: *discipled*) by Christ, John lost the rough edges of his personality. He was no longer brash and offensive. He was still courageous, but he also learned to be gentle. He had all of his passion, but the anger was replaced with compassion. Consider some of John's other personality traits:

- *He had been violent.* Jesus had to calm him down after a Samaritan village spurned Christ's ministry. John blew his stack and asked Jesus if he should call down fire from heaven to destroy the village. (See Luke 9:52-56.)

- *He had been overbearing.* When someone who wasn't one of the 12 disciples was driving out demons, John tried to stop him because "he isn't in our group." (See Luke 9:49-50.)

- *He had been self-centered.* He asked Jesus to give him a seat of honor right beside Christ in heaven. As you can imagine, this act of self-promotion didn't go over very well with the rest of the 12 disciples. (See Mark 10:35-41.)

Yet, later in his life, these offensive personality traits were gone. In their place was a humility that prevented him from even using his own name in his Gospel. Even though he was Christ's closest friend, John never once mentions his own name. Only John's encounter with Christ can explain this type of transformation.

Of course, you'll be missing the whole point of John if you don't personally respond to the obvious questions: Who do you think Jesus is? And if you believe Him to be God, what are you doing about it?

Study the Word

1. Before you start an intense chapter-by-chapter study
    of John, read through the entire Gospel. Do it
    quickly to get an overall impression. As you read,
    watch for these things:

    - the *words* of Christ in which He claimed to be
      God

    - the *actions* of Christ that revealed His supernat-
      ural nature

    - the *reactions* of people as they encountered Christ

2. What are the clues that John was a close friend of
    Christ? What evidence in your life shows that you are
    a close friend of Christ? Give some specifics.

3. You are part of the audience to whom John was
    writing (although we are sure that he didn't imagine
    and couldn't comprehend how you could download
    his Gospel off the Internet). So you'll be encoun-
    tering Christ as you read John. You won't have a
    face-to-face encounter, but we're sure that Christ will
    meet with you through the words that John wrote.
    That means you may experience a little transformation
    as you comprehend more of who Christ is. And that's

exactly what John was hoping would happen to you. Here are a few questions to think about before you begin your more detailed study of John:

• What is your impression of Christ right now?

• How well do you think you know Him?

• What aspects of your personality may be transformed as you get to know more about Christ?

4. The Gospel of John may change your impressions about the people you will be reading about. At this point, describe your understanding of the personalities of...

• Jesus

• John

• Peter

• Judas

• the Pharisees

5. In your answer to question 5 of chapter 1, you told
    what you knew about John. After reading chapter 2,
    has your opinion of him changed? How?

Chapter 3

[John] is the most unusual gospel, with its distinct content and style. It is easily the simplest and yet the most profound of the Gospels. And for many people it is the greatest and most powerful. John writes his Gospel for the specific purpose of bringing people to spiritual life through belief in the person and work of Jesus Christ.

—*Bruce Wilkinson & Kenneth Boa*

$\mathcal{B}$eginning $\mathcal{B}$efore the $\mathcal{B}$eginning

If you were writing a biography about a person, you would probably start the story at the birth of the individual. Maybe you would go a little further back in time, just to bring in the ancestral lineage. That's what Matthew did in his Gospel. He went back into Christ's genealogy as far as Abraham, and he traced the family tree down from Abraham to Joseph (the husband of Mary, the mother of Jesus).

John wasn't interested in genealogies, but he goes back even further in time than Matthew did. John starts his Gospel by going back to a time before the world existed.

INCARNATION: God Gets Down to Earth

John 1:1-18

*W*hat's *A*head

- ☐ Say the Word (John 1:1-3)

- ☐ Letting In the Light (John 1:4-18)

*J*ohn doesn't waste any time getting to his point that Jesus is God. He hammers on that theme at the very outset of his Gospel. But interestingly, he doesn't mention Jesus by name right away. Instead, John refers to Christ as "the Word," "the light," and "the Son of God." Don't worry if this seems confusing to you. It *is* confusing (although a little background information will clear it up for you). And don't worry about the rest of the Gospel. Most of the mysterious stuff is right at the beginning, so things will get easier as you read along.

Say the Word (John 1:1-3)

Remember that John's audience included both Greeks and Jews. The Greeks prided themselves on their intellectual ability, and John would have to appeal to them on that basis. With the Jews, John was going to have to present his arguments in the context of Jewish history and the role of the Messiah. By referring to Christ as "the Word" in John 1:1 and following, John was killing two theological birds with one stone:

- The Greek term for *word (logos)* had a definition that encompassed reason, order, and rational thought. In a sense, it represented the mind of God that brought structure to the natural world and to the thinking processes of humanity.

- The Jews would recognize a reference to *word* in the context of the Word of God. They knew that God spoke the world into existence (Genesis 1:3) and were familiar with all of the instances in which the prophets of Israel had spoken "the word of the Lord."

John manages to get the attention of both the Greek and the Jew when he begins his Gospel by referring to Jesus as "the Word." And he makes his point that Jesus is God by emphasizing that Jesus existed before the world was created.

In the beginning the Word already existed. He was with God, and he was God (John 1:1).

As if that wasn't enough, John underscores Christ's God-nature by stating that Jesus was responsible for the creation of the world.

He created everything there is. Nothing exists that he didn't make (John 1:3).

John's references to both a spiritual world and a physical world would be in complete agreement with the

Greeks as well as the Jews. The Greeks believed in the dual reality of two worlds (which Plato referred to as the perfect unseen world and the imperfect present world).

Letting in the Light (John 1:4-18)

John presents God's entire salvation story in this first short section of his Gospel. But he does it in a skillful way by making a transition in his references. Look at the progression that John uses. He takes "the Word" from the outer reaches of the universe and brings Him down to earth as a means of salvation for humanity. Notice how he gets through the entire story line without mentioning the name of Jesus:

- The Word was in the beginning (1:1).

- The Word created life (1:4).

- The Life gives light to everyone (1:4).

- The light shines in the darkness (1:5).

- John the Baptist told people that the light was coming to earth (1:9).

- When the light came to earth, His own people rejected Him (1:10-11).

- Those who believed in Him received spiritual rebirth from God (1:12-13).

John recaps this progression in verse 14 by saying that the Word came to earth in the form of human flesh and was the Son of God. And then in verse 17, John delivers the punch line that this person is Jesus Christ.

$\mathcal{B}$elieve $\mathcal{I}$t or $\mathcal{N}$ot

John is only 12 verses into his Gospel when he hits on his favorite theme of how people—including you—respond to Jesus. Yes, some of His contemporaries rejected Jesus (see John 1:11), but not all of them. Some of them believed Him and accepted Him (John 1:12), and these became "children of God."

Everyone is a child of God in the sense that God created humans and is responsible for giving us life. But that isn't the connection that John is referring to. In this passage he is talking about those who get to know Christ in an intimate, personal, and eternal relationship. Verses 11 and 12 reveal the difference between those who rejected Him and those whom He considers His "children." The difference involves belief. Believing and accepting that Christ is the Savior separates those who merely know of Him from those who are part of His family.

The importance of belief in Christ can't be overstated. Maybe that's why John emphasizes it all throughout his Gospel and then concludes with a statement that encouraging your belief in Christ as the Savior was his purpose in writing the Gospel (see John 20:30-31).

Read the first 18 verses of John and notice how simply the entire salvation story is presented.

The story is simple, but some of the theological concepts can never be fully comprehended by mere mortals. For instance, John 1:14 says that "the Word became human." Entire books have been written about this verse. When Christ came to earth, He was not solely human like the rest of us. But He wasn't a half-breed either, being part man and part God. Christ was all God and all man at the same time. (See Colossians 2:9.)

$\mathcal{S}$tudy the $\mathcal{W}$ord

1. God "gave us His Word." What does that tell you about Jesus?

2. What was Jesus' role in the creation of the world? See John 1:3 and Colossians 1:15-17. Notice the plural references to God in the creation account (Genesis 1:26).

3. In what way does Jesus, the light, shine through the darkness?

4. What does John mean when he says Jesus gives light to everyone?

5. What are the ramifications of the incarnation?

Chapter 4

Two of the constantly recurring
themes of this Gospel are the nature of the
unbelief that led the Jews to refuse to accept
Jesus as the Messiah, and the prerequisites
and constituent factors of the faith that led
His disciples to acknowledge Him as the One
"of whom Moses in the law, and the
prophets, did write."

—*R.V.G. Tasker*

The Real Deal

Having established Jesus as God, John now moves his narrative into real-life instances of people coming face-to-face with Jesus. Remember that the Jews are anxiously awaiting the arrival of the Messiah. But don't think that this led them to wholeheartedly embrace Christ as the long-expected Savior. As you'll see, He received a mixed reception of belief and unbelief.

PRESENTATION: Introducing Jesus to the World

John 1:19–4:54

What's Ahead

- ☐ John the Baptist (John 1:19-34; 3:22-36)

- ☐ Jesus Cleans House at the Temple (John 2:13-22)

- ☐ Nicodemus, the Midnight Visitor (John 3:1-21)

- ☐ The Samaritan Woman (John 4)

*I*n this passage, you will see Jesus launch His public ministry. John the Baptist opens the action by pronouncing that Jesus is the Messiah. With that coronation, Jesus immediately becomes the object of scrutiny. Those who are critical watch Him, and those who are curious follow Him.

By selectively reporting and emphasizing what Jesus said as well as what He did, John shows how Jesus began His ministry with a blend of...

- teaching—to present the truth of God

- miracles—to reveal His power as God

As you read through the passage, watch for the shifts between action and explanation. This must have been a powerful and convincing combination. As you will read, it was enough to cause some men to shift their allegiance from John the Baptist to Jesus. Christ's presence and power were enough to cause some to leave their jobs and follow Him.

John the Baptist (John 1:19-34; 3:22-36)

Here's a little insight about the relationship between John the Baptist and Jesus. They were second cousins (their mothers were first cousins). They were close in age—John the Baptist was about six months older than Jesus. They probably knew each other as children. Imagine how their childhood friendship might have affected their relationship as adults when John the Baptist declared his younger cousin to be the Messiah.

John the Baptist had a large and loyal following long before Jesus began His public ministry. The populous loved John the Baptist's fearless attacks on the hypocrisy of the Jewish leaders. They recognized him as a prophet who spoke for God. Remember that John was originally a follower of John the Baptist.

No jealousy existed between John the Baptist and Jesus. Notice as you read the passage of 1:19-34 that John the Baptist clearly understood his God-given role of directing people's attention to the Messiah. Unfortunately, his own disciples were not as gracious or perceptive. The disciples of John the Baptist got jealous when they heard that Jesus and His disciples were also baptizing people as part of a ceremonial display of repentance and cleansing of sin. Notice in 3:22-36 how John the Baptist diffuses the competitiveness of his own disciples by reiterating the undeniable fact that Jesus was the Messiah, the only way of salvation.

By the time the Gospel of John was being written, perhaps 60 years after both Jesus and John the Baptist had died, a segment within the Jewish Christian community continued to give inappropriate regard to the role of John the Baptist. (See Acts 19:1-7 as an example.) In other words, they were worshiping the memory of John the Baptist instead of giving full devotion to Christ. As he wrote his Gospel, John had to deal with this issue. He wouldn't want to discredit or disrespect his former mentor, John the Baptist. But he needed to make clear John the Baptist's subservience to Christ. Notice how artfully John handles this subject by quoting the extensive comments of John the Baptist that raise up Christ without giving any attention to himself.

We can learn a lot from the humility of John the Baptist. In the chain of famous Christians, he would be near the top. Yet as you read the text of John, you never see John the Baptist taking any credit or grabbing the spotlight. Often in our Christian lives, we are glad to give God the glory, but we enjoy receiving accolades for the things He has accomplished through us. Let's learn a lesson from John the Baptist. It's all about Christ.

The Wedding at Cana
(John 2:1-12)

The fascinating thing about the Gospel of John is the story behind every story. John didn't feel obligated to talk about every event and detail of Christ's life (since most of the facts had been covered in the Synoptic Gospels). Consequently, he was selective about what he chose to include, and he always had a reason behind the events that made the cut.

For example, on the few occasions when John reports on a miracle, he is always primarily interested in exposing the response of the people who witnessed it. Sometimes people saw the miracle but refused the obvious conclusion that Jesus was God. Other times the miracle was the tipping point that caused them to believe in Christ.

And that is apparently the reason that John chose to include this obscure miracle of Jesus turning the water into wine at a humble wedding in Cana. Notice that Jesus didn't bring attention to what He did. Only the servants and disciples knew what happened. Yet John makes a point of saying that this was the first display of Christ's glory, and it was the event that triggered the disciples' belief in Him (2:11).

Jesus Cleans House at the Temple (John 2:13-22)

This is an interesting passage that requires a little cultural background to be understood properly. On your initial reading, it might appear as if Jesus is some type of (a) crazed lunatic or (b) violent rabble-rouser or (c) religious fanatic. Even giving Him the benefit of the doubt, the image of Him waving a whip in the Temple suggests that He lost control of His temper. So, how does this fit with Jesus being the sinless Son of God?

To understand Jesus' response of righteous indignation, you have to know how the Temple economy worked. It was a corrupt system to be sure. Here is how the scam played out:

- Passover was a sacred holiday during which Jews from all over the world made a pilgrimage to Jerusalem.

- When the Jews visited the Temple, they were required to pay a Temple tax that amounted to about two days' wages. But the Temple tax could only be paid in acceptable Temple money. Since most of the Jews were from outside the area, they needed to exchange their currency for Temple coins.

- The "money changers" were gouging the people with excessive fees. They would charge a handling fee equivalent to one day's wage just to make the currency exchange.

- The money changers paid a kickback to the Jewish religious authorities who were in charge of the Temple. This payola represented a huge source of income for the priests.

But the money-grubbing priests weren't satisfied with their kickbacks, and their money-gouging techniques weren't limited to Temple tax exchange rates. They came up with other income-producing schemes:

- People were required to present an animal to be sacrificed by the priest on their behalf.

- The out-of-towners had to buy an animal on the Temple premises because they couldn't carry one in their luggage.

- Most local residents had to purchase a sacrificial animal at the Temple, too. The priests usually "disqualified" an animal brought from home as being less than perfect. The locals had about as much luck getting an animal into the Temple as you would have trying to sneak two dozen Krispy Kreme doughnuts into a movie theater.

- As you might guess, the priests sold the sacrificial animals at the Temple at exorbitant prices. And to make matters worse, the animals were often flawed or crippled (which violated the criteria for an animal sacrifice). But the priests wanted to make an extra shekel or two or twenty, so they bought damaged merchandise at a discount and resold it at a jacked-up price.

These merchandising operations were the primary activity in the Temple. The priests were allowing commercial transactions to expand beyond the general courtyards and into the areas reserved for prayer.

Jesus responded to these flagrant abuses. Just like you would swat at an infectious, diseased rodent with a broom to get it out of your home, Jesus swatted at a few Jewish leaders because they were desecrating the holiness of the Temple. This was not a case in which Jesus lost His temper. He just took care of business.

Nicodemus, the Midnight Visitor (John 3:1-21)

The encounter between Jesus and Nicodemus was no ordinary encounter. Nicodemus was a Pharisee. The Pharisees were a high-ranking order in the Jewish social hierarchy. They prided themselves on their ability to keep all of the nitpicky religious laws they had enacted. (God's Ten Commandments and the other rules and regulations weren't enough for them. They created an entire set of additional regulations that were impossible to follow in real life except for those who led the privileged life of a Pharisee.)

Pharisees believed that they were God's favorites because they kept all of the regulations.

The disciples must have been astonished that a Pharisee would want to have a sincere Q & A session with Jesus. Like John the Baptist, Jesus was upsetting the Jewish social order by proclaiming that God was more interested in the condition of a person's heart than his adherence to the rules and regulations.

Think about the dynamics of this encounter as you read this passage. Nicodemus would suffer horrendous consequences if his fellow Pharisees discovered he met with Jesus. (Consequently, he and Jesus had a clandestine meeting in the middle of the night.) Yet Nicodemus' heart was so sincere, and Christ was so compelling, that Nicodemus was willing to take the risk.

Fortunately for us, Nicodemus was spiritually dense. His questions prompted Jesus' prolonged explanations about the simplicity of salvation. But let's not be too harsh in our treatment of Nicodemus. After all, he had spent a lifetime trying to earn favor with God. Now he was being told that salvation was a simple matter of belief in Christ. How about you? In these 21 verses, you have read the same explanation that Nicodemus heard. But are you still trying to earn a position in heaven by keeping rules and regulations?

Do you feel under an obligation to do religious activities? Are you taking pride in your spiritual accomplishments? Do you, like Nicodemus, think your position with God is based on how perfect you are? Salvation and your relationship with God are not about your achievements but rather about what Christ did for you on the cross. Follow Nicodemus' example and spend some one-on-one time with Christ as you reread this passage. (And you don't even have to wait until midnight to do it.)

The Samaritan Woman (John 4)

Here is another story behind the story, and the factual background amplifies an already intriguing encounter between Jesus and the Samaritan woman. Here's a little bit of what was going on behind the scene:

- Palestine is configured in a long and skinny shape. It is about 120 miles long from north to south. It is divided up into three sections: Galilee in the north, Samaria in the middle, and Judea in the south.

- Jesus had been in Judea, but the Pharisees there were getting upset that so many people were following Him. In fact, Christ's disciples were baptizing more followers than John the Baptist. The Pharisees could barely tolerate John the Baptist, but they didn't want this upstart Jesus to be even more successful with the people. Jesus wanted to avoid the controversy at this time, so He decided to leave Judea and head north to Galilee (4:1-3).

- The direct route to Galilee went through Samaria. But the Jews despised the Samaritans. The Jews considered them to be half-breeds, and there was a long-standing feud between the Jews and the Samaritans. Each group hated the other.

- Most Jews never traveled through Samaria. Instead, they walked around it. Skirting around Samaria required three extra days of travel, but the Jews were willing to spend the extra time and energy because their hatred for the Samaritans was so great.

- Finally, Jewish customs forbade a man from talking to a woman in public.

With this historical and cultural background, now read the passage. To get the full impact of John's message, notice that...

- Jesus was human and got tired and thirsty.

- Jesus broke through the barriers of nationalism by going through Samaria.

- Jesus must have already had a tremendous influence on His disciples because they went into a Samaritan village and talked with Samaritans as they purchased food.

- Jesus rejected ridiculous social customs and spoke with the woman.

- Jesus never wasted an opportunity to bring a conversation around to spiritual matters.

- Jesus revealed His supernatural nature by knowing the facts of this woman's shady past.

- The woman is quick to change the subject when Jesus confronts her immoral lifestyle, but Jesus brings the conversation back to the topic of salvation.

True to his style, John doesn't leave the story without showing the woman's response to her encounter with Christ. Even though she was a moral outcast, her testimony prompted others in the village to come to Christ. Their encounter with Him left them convinced that He was "the Savior of the world" (4:42).

*H*ealing an *O*fficial's *S*on
(John 4:43-54)

This section concludes with a miracle. All miracles are amazing, but since John includes so few of them, you have to wonder what made this miracle so special that he chose to report it. Our suspicion is that John wanted to show that Christ's power was not confined to dimensions of time and space. As you read this account of divine healing, notice that Jesus was not even in the same place as the person He healed. How do you think this event influenced the disciples' impression of Jesus?

■ ■ ■

*S*tudy the *W*ord

1. Read through John 1:15-34 and 3:22-36. Identify statements made by John the Baptist about Christ's supremacy.

2. When Jesus turned the water into wine (John 2:1-12), what would have been the impact on these people?

   • Jesus' mother

- the servants

- the steward of the feast

- the disciples

3. In one phrase, what was Jesus so upset about when He drove the money changers from the Temple (John 2:13-22)?

4. The conversation with Nicodemus (found only in the Gospel of John) gives John another opportunity to present the whole plan of salvation to his readers. See how many separate explanations of salvation you can find in the passage. We'll get you started with a few of them:

    - the explanation of being "born again"

    - the reference to the bronze snake (The story is told in Numbers 21. The Israelites escaped physical death by looking at a snake on a pole. We look to Jesus on the cross to deliver us from spiritual death.)

    - the explanation of the Gospel message contained in the single verse of John 3:16

5. Jesus spoke with a woman—a Samaritan woman! Who are the "Samaritan women" (social outcasts) that the church in America could reach out to today?

6. Put yourself back in time about 2000 years, and pretend that you were a bystander who witnessed all of the events and discussions in John 1:19–4:54. Would you be persuaded that Jesus was the Son of God? If yes, was there anything in particular that convinced you? If no, what additional proof or explanations would you need?

Would you be willing to put your life on hold and follow Jesus if He called you to be a disciple along with Peter, Andrew, and the rest of the guys? What would hold you back? What misgivings would you have about going? About declining His offer and staying at home?

These questions aren't as hypothetical as you may think. Christ is calling you to be His disciple. He wants you to leave behind your extra baggage and follow Him. Are you following Him with enthusiasm? Is anything holding you back?

*C*hapter 5

We learn much in life by asking questions,
and this greatest of all questions has much
to teach us. All the pressing questions and
problems of today are secondary to the
pointed question, "What think ye of
Christ?" Answer this, and you find the
answers to other questions.

—*Herbert Lockyer*

Refusing to Believe

Up to this point in his Gospel, John has been weaving in a theme that the Jews would reject Jesus as the Messiah. Have you picked up on references such as these?

- *Even in his own land and among his own people, he was not accepted* (1:11).

- *The light from heaven came into the world, but they loved the darkness more than the light, for their actions were evil. They hate the light because they want to sin in the darkness* (3:19-20).

- *He has come from above and is greater than anyone else....He tells what he has seen and heard, but how few believe what he tells them* (3:31-32).

In this section of four chapters, John is going to hammer hard on the point that the Jews openly opposed Christ even though He was faultless and continually displayed sufficient proof that He is the Messiah. We will cover some of the highlights of this section to give you some background insights. But the point of what you read in John 5–8 will be obvious to you. Time after time, Jesus revealed that He was God through the things that He did and the words that He spoke. The Jews had no lack of evidence. Yet, they opposed Him because they did not want to submit to His authority.

EVALUATION: Confronting the Obvious

John 5–8

*A*s you read these four chapters in John, you might be amazed that people could be so stubborn. How could they refuse to follow Christ when His authority as God was so apparent? That's a good question for each of us to ask ourselves. Can we read John 5–8 and still resist shifting control of our lives over to Jesus? Could we possibly have knowledge of who Christ is and yet not receive Him? Is our faith often weak even though we have witnessed His power? Reading John 5–8 isn't just an opportunity to observe human nature in others. These chapters will force you to analyze your own level of commitment to Christ whether you want to or not.

Criticism for Healing a Lame Man (John 5)

This episode is an excellent example of the opposition that confronted Jesus. If you think that the healing of a man who had been crippled for 38 years would be a cause for citywide celebration, you're wrong. Actually, the man was elated, but the religious authorities were ticked off.

As we previously discussed, the Jewish leaders had taken God's basic laws and principles and manipulated them into thousands of rules and regulations. For example, God had given Moses the law that said no work should be performed on the Sabbath. The Jewish leaders had stretched the interpretation so far as to prohibit carrying a sewing needle in the pocket of your robe on the Sabbath. They weren't such weaklings that they considered carrying a needle to be heavy work. No, they were just way overzealous in their attempt to protect God's laws. Even though their interpretation seems ridiculous, if you were found guilty of intentionally carrying something on the Sabbath, your punishment could be death by stoning.

Jesus just happened to heal this lame man on the Sabbath, and the religious leaders caught the man dancing down the street *carrying* his mattress. In his own defense, the man explained that he was carrying the mattress because Jesus had told him to. This gave the Jewish leaders the ammunition they wanted to harass Jesus. Jesus turned the tables on them and went on the offensive by giving a sermon that offended them even more. As you read this passage, notice the things that Jesus said that ticked off the religious leaders:

- His first response was that God never stops working, so neither does He. He was equating His work with the work of God.

- He referred to Himself as God's Son.

- He clearly positioned Himself as the Messiah.

- He claimed the power to raise the dead.

- He declared Himself to be their Judge.

The religious leaders didn't care about the truth of these claims. They just wanted Jesus stopped because He was a threat to them. After all, He disregarded the rules for the sake of compassion. What a rebel!

Bread and Water (John 6)

Remember that the first century A.D. was a time before fast-food franchises. This presented a problem for the people who followed Christ in search of healing and miracles. This passage begins with the story of Christ's miracle of feeding thousands of people by multiplying the contents of a boy's bag lunch.

Walking on the Water
(John 6:16-21)

In verses 16-21, you'll find the famous miracle of Christ walking on the water. This is the abbreviated version. You can find an expanded narrative in Matthew 14:22-33 and Mark 6:45-52. Those accounts indicate that Jesus desired to be alone for a while, and He sent His disciples ahead in the boat to the nearby lakeside village of Capernaum. They battled for hours against a raging storm but couldn't reach the shore. Then Jesus came walking to them on the water. When He sat in the boat, they safely reached their destination.

Interestingly, the disciples were doing exactly what Jesus said when they encountered the storm. God may have intended that entire incident so they could witness God's power over the forces of nature, and Christ's presence with them in the storm. And that's what God wants us to realize as well. Our lives will not be storm-free simply because we are following Jesus, but He will always be present with us.

In Search of a Free Lunch (John 6:22-71)

The Jews were living under Roman oppression. Although they could have their own religious form of government, they were subject to the rule of Rome (and all its taxes). This military, political, and social tyranny made the people anticipate the promised Messiah. Jesus was the Messiah, and the people were anxious for the Messiah's arrival, so why didn't Jesus cater to them?

This passage illustrates that Jesus knew the people were not sincere in their adoration of Him. They loved Him as long as He was feeding them and healing them for free. They would follow Him anywhere for a free lunch.

But Jesus explained that following Him required a personal commitment. People got uneasy. They liked the freebies, but they didn't want to make a personal sacrifice. But sacrifice is what being a Christian is all about. Jesus made this plain in 6:53-58 as He used terminology that was common to animal sacrifices. (For us twenty-first-century readers, this passage seems a little cannibalistic. If you had grown up with the custom of gutting a goat on an altar, however, these references wouldn't make you squeamish.)

We can be critical of the crowds who followed Jesus because they treated Him like a holy vending machine. They were only interested in Him for what they could get out of Him. But do we fall into the same trap every once in a while? Do we get super-spiritual when we need something from God, but ignore Him when things are going fine? Are we interested in what God can get out of us, or are we more concerned about what we can get out of God?

Guessing Games at the Festival (John 7)

The events of this chapter occur during one of the Jews' annual festivals. It was the Festival of Tabernacles (or Festival of Shelters) that was held at the end of September and the beginning of October each year. Attendance was mandatory for all adult males who lived within a 15-mile radius of Jerusalem, but all devoted Jews would attend if they were able to do so.

In chapter 7, John underscores his theme of examining the responses of the people to Jesus. In each instance, you can judge for yourself whether their unbelief was based on the evidence or some other underlying motivation:

- *Ridicule* (7:1-9). Jesus' own brother (half-brothers, actually, as they shared only the same mother) were quite sarcastic towards Him.

- *Fear* (7:10-13). The people were honestly curious about Christ, but open debate was stifled. No one was brave enough to speak a positive word about Him in public. They seemed to be more afraid of the religious leaders than they were of God Himself.

- ***Opposition*** (7:14-24). The Jewish officials couldn't stand the fact that Jesus spoke with such authority and knowledge but hadn't gone through their rigorous educational programs. They had to resort to name-calling, and they chose to label Him as being demon possessed.

- ***Cowardice*** (7:25-52). With a portion of the general public awakening to the fact that Jesus was the Messiah, the Jewish leaders became desperate. They felt they could only stop Christ's growing popularity if they silenced Him. But they didn't have the guts to do it themselves, so they sent the Temple guards to arrest Him. Big mistake. These guards, apparently being open-minded men, were persuaded by the person and words of Christ. They couldn't bring themselves to arrest Him.

They Don't Know What They Don't Know (John 8)

John makes a slight shift in his theme as he moves from chapter 7 to chapter 8. In the prior chapter he clearly established that most of the Jews had no real clue about who Jesus was. Through Christ's discourse in chapter 8, John reveals that they had very little understanding about theological matters as well. So they didn't know about the person of Jesus, and they didn't understand His purpose in God's great plan.

Watch how the ignorance of the people regarding spiritual matters is revealed throughout the chapter:

- *verses 1-11:* They were blind to the significance of their own sin. They were quick to condemn the woman who was sleeping around, but they paid no attention to their own sins (until Jesus made them think about their own guilt).

- *verses 12-20:* The religious leaders were trying to judge and evaluate Him according to human standards. This was impossible to do because He had a divine origin.

- *verses 21-30:* They did not understand the fundamental principle in God's plan that required the sacrificial death of the Messiah.

- *verses 31-47:* Even those who professed to believe in Him later proved to be faithless. They simply did not understand that freedom is attained by acknowledging that Christ is the truth for all life.

- *verses 48-59:* They didn't understand Christ's distinctions between physical death and spiritual death.

And the people also didn't understand that God was in control of the timing of Christ's death. Their premature attempts to murder Jesus always failed (8:59). His death was certain, but it would happen at the time and in the way God planned.

$\mathcal{S}$tudy the $\mathcal{W}$ord

1. When Jesus healed the lame man on the Sabbath (John 5), the man was overjoyed, but the Jewish leaders were furious. Why were their responses so different?

2. Why did the 5000 that Jesus fed (John 6) continue to seek Him for a while? What motivation would Jesus prefer that they had?

3. John 7 shows the confusion and controversy that followed Jesus wherever He went. People couldn't figure Him out. The guards who were sent to arrest Him were so confounded by what He said that they abandoned their assignment. Was He the Messiah or not? Was He a bad guy, as the Jewish leaders made Him out to be? Were His miracles legit or fakes? As you read John 7, list the following:

    *   each reference to someone who was plotting against Jesus

- each person (or group) that was pressuring Him to do something

- each emotion that Jesus evoked in the people

- each opinion as to His character or identity

- each statement made by Jesus as to who He was

Do you think that Jesus is more controversial today than He was almost 2000 years ago, or less?

4. In John 8, the Jews are still very confused about Jesus. In each of these sections, what seems to be hindering the people from coming to the light, and what is Jesus' recommendation to them?

   • 8:12-20

   • 8:21-30

   • 8:31-48

   • 8:49-59

5. In John 8:34-38, Jesus talks about being a slave to sin. What does this mean?

Chapter 6

"I am the gate," Jesus says..."I am the good shepherd." Jews who hear those words undoubtedly think back to Old Testament kings like David, who are known as the shepherds of Israel....As he [Jesus] explains, a truly good shepherd, unlike a hired hand, "lays down his life for the sheep." He is the only person in history who chooses to be born, chooses to die, and chooses to come back again.

—*Philip Yancey*

$\mathcal{P}$op $\mathcal{Q}$uiz

Think back over the previous eight chapters you have read in John. How many miracles can you think of? And don't even count the ones that only the disciples saw—just name the ones that Jesus performed in public.

Don't you think that these miracles would have been enough to convince you that Jesus was believable, or at least that His message was worth further consideration?

You are about to read four chapters in which Christ makes it clear to any objective person that He has the power and authority to back up His claims. And, in so doing, He presents Himself in four separate roles that the people could easily identify. Like Him or not, He was going to leave no doubt about who He was and what He was all about.

IDENTIFICATION: Leaving No Doubt

John 9–12

Chapters 9–12 of John present miracles of Christ that are correlated with aspects of Messiahship. The Jews thought the Messiah would rescue them from the military tyranny of the Roman Empire. That was a misguided notion. Christ wanted to expand their concept of the Messiah into spiritual and eternal realms. Thus, in the following chapters He presents Himself to the people as...

- • chapter 9—The Sight-Giver

- • chapter 10—The Shepherd

- chapter 11—The Life-Giver

- chapter 12—The King

Even the Blind Man Could See It (John 9)

Jesus performed this miracle to prove that He was God. How do we know? Because that is what Jesus said. The theological question presented to Jesus was whether the man's blindness (which he had since birth) was the fault of his sin or his parents' sin. (The question presupposed that God imposed illness as a punishment for sin.) Jesus said that the blindness was not related to sin but was intended to reveal God's power. And after speaking those words, Christ proved that He was God by curing the man's blindness.

Don't miss the rich character studies in the rest of the story. Aside from Jesus, you've got...

> ***The Disciples:*** Their role is small but significant. They saw a blind man, and they asked whether his handicap was due to his sin or the sin of his parents. (The prevailing view at the time was that birth defects were either the result of the parents' sin or the infant's prenatal sin—a bizarre concept.) Jesus answers their question by indicating no relationship between the suffering and sin. Instead, He said the purpose was to glorify God.

> ***The Blind Man:*** Perhaps his blindness had given him strength of character over the years. He didn't cave in to the pressure from the Pharisees. He stood strong in defense of the miracle that Christ had performed. And he wasn't satisfied with just

physical healing; he pursued Christ for spiritual answers as well.

The Blind Man's Parents: Although their son was fearless, they were fearful. But you can hardly blame them. They knew that giving credit to Jesus for a miracle would mean offending the Pharisees. If that happened, they could be excommunicated from the synagogue. They panicked, and they deflected the interrogation back to their son.

The Pharisees: What a bunch of desperate guys. They went to great lengths to disprove the miracle. Although everyone had known this man to be blind since birth, they hauled in his parents for questioning. Apparently they were hoping to coerce a phony confession that the man had been faking blindness all of those years. And they couldn't respond in a rational manner to the arguments that the man presented. They had to resort to abuse, insults, and threats.

Blindness still existed at the end of the chapter, but not in the eyes of the man. The Pharisees were blind in a spiritual sense. They were blind to the fact that Jesus was the Messiah. Jesus tried to make them realize His point, but they couldn't see it.

Sheep in Need of a Shepherd (John 10)

Although the people might have been confused about Jesus, they knew their Old Testament (which wasn't the *Old* Testament to them but was their sacred writings). They knew, for example, that the image of a shepherd was used by the prophets of old to represent the Messiah, who would come to care for His people. (See Isaiah 40:11 and Ezekiel 34:23.) Anyone familiar with these prophecies would know exactly what Jesus meant when He stated that He was the promised "good shepherd."

In the first part of chapter 10, Jesus refers to Himself as the shepherd and the people as the sheep. Look at the relationship between the two:

- The sheep come to the shepherd.

- The shepherd knows each sheep by name.

- The sheep follow the shepherd as he leads them.

- The shepherd protects his sheep from thieves and robbers who would harm them.

Perhaps the greatest attribute of a shepherd is that he is willing to give his life for the sheep. Shepherd kept their sheep at night in a sheepfold, which was a fenced area with only one narrow opening. The shepherd slept in the opening. If a wild animal or a robber sought to attack the sheep, the shepherd would be in the way. With this background, Christ stated that He would lay down His life for His sheep.

Notice the affirmative context of verses 11-18. Jesus claimed that He would willingly lay down His life. Although the people didn't fully realize what He was saying, Jesus knew of His impending death. But it was not going to be a victim's death. He was voluntarily going to be the sacrifice for the sake of His sheep.

How's Your Shepherd?

Is John getting his message across to you? He wants you to understand that the single most important question in life is, How are you going to respond to Jesus? He often highlights this issue by contrasting what Jesus says about Himself with what others say about Him. Sometimes people agree with Jesus that He is the Son of God. Many times they don't. John 10 gives another example of Christ clearly explaining His role (this time, in the metaphor of a loving shepherd who would risk his life for his sheep), while in the background, the Jewish leaders pursue their plots to kill Him. How do you respond to the One who wants to be your Shepherd?

The last part of this chapter, verses 19-42, focuses on the disbelief of the Jewish leaders. They understood Him correctly when He stated that He and the Father are one. They plotted to kill Him for making such a statement.

Dead Man Walking (John 11)

Jesus had already claimed to have power over death and the ability to grant eternal life. Now He took another opportunity to prove that death was no obstacle for Him.

You will notice that when Jesus received the message that His good friend, Lazarus, was dying, He didn't rush to help him. Instead, Jesus seemed to stall before leaving. Many scholars believe that Christ intentionally delayed His departure to Bethany so that Lazarus would die in the meantime. Jesus wasn't being sadistic. He knew that no calamity could befall Lazarus that He couldn't remedy. And the end result was the miraculous act of raising Lazarus from the dead, which glorified God and further established Christ's credentials as the Messiah.

As in other occasions, the miracle isn't the high point of this chapter. Rather, the miracle simply illustrates the point Jesus was making. In this chapter, the focal point is Christ's statement to Martha in verse 25: "I am the resurrection and the life. Those who believe in me, even though they die like everyone else, will live again." Of course, if Christ claims to have power over death and the power to grant eternal life, then He ought to prove it. So He did, and Lazarus came walking out of the burial cave.

This was an amazing event that couldn't be denied. Even the chief priests and the Pharisees acknowledged that Jesus was performing "many miraculous signs." But their hearts were hardened against Jesus, and they began to plot His death.

Trust God's Timing

Have you been noticing how Jesus controls His activities and timetable? He is focused on His goal—the cross. He doesn't let other people dictate a schedule that will interfere with His primary mission and timeline. Further evidence of that is presented in chapter 11:

- Mary and Martha wanted Jesus to drop what He was doing and rush to Bethany to cure Lazarus. But Jesus waited a few days before going.

- The disciples didn't want Jesus to go back to Bethany in the region of Judea because Jesus had received death threats there. Jesus went anyway.

- The High Priest, Caiaphas, and the Pharisees plotted the assassination of Jesus. Christ thwarted their plans and left the area because He knew that wasn't supposed to be the time or manner of His death.

We can learn an important lesson from this. We will never be able to demand or dictate what God is supposed to do. We can express our opinions. God wants us in constant dialogue with Him (spiritual term: *prayer*). But like the disciples, after we express our opinion, we must be ready to follow God if He leads us in a direction we didn't want to go. Trust God's timing and direction. He sees the big picture.

Perfume, a Parade, and a Bombshell (John 12)

Notice the three contrasting segments in this passage. Chapter 12 begins with a very precious scene as Mary anoints Jesus' feet with perfume. Although Mary's behavior might be a little strange in our culture, at that time her actions were considered a sign of respect, worship, and adoration. Perhaps Mary's conduct can teach us something about how we should worship God. If you follow her pattern, then your worship will be...

> *Centered on Christ:* He was the sole focus of her attention. She wasn't distracted by anyone around her (even though the room must have been crowded). She wasn't worried about what anybody thought about her (even though she had critics in the room). She didn't draw attention away from Christ. She just sat quietly and humbly at His feet and made Him the center of her world. Can the same be said of our worship? Are we fully focused on Christ when we worship Him, or are we thinking about other things at the same time? Are we worshiping humbly, or are we getting a little attention ourselves?

> *Costly to You:* Mary didn't anoint Christ's feet with cheap cologne from a free sample that she

got in the mail. She used expensive perfume. Scholars have determined that the cost of it would have been equivalent to the wages a man could have earned in one year. Our worship may not have a financial impact, but it may be costly to us in terms of our time (which may be a more precious commodity to us). Are you willing to expend your time to give God the worship He deserves each day?

Criticized by Others: Judas didn't have a sincere love of Christ, so he was critical of Mary's worship. Other people may be critical of you if you make worshiping God a priority in your life. They may want your time or attention, and they will object if you put them behind God. Who do you care about the most? Are you going to be deterred by the critics, or are you going to worship Christ?

From the private moment with Mary, the scene shifts to a parade down Main Street in Jerusalem. This is the Triumphal Entry, which is commemorated by Christians on Palm Sunday. The city was crowded with people who had made the pilgrimage to Jerusalem for the annual celebration of Passover. The city's population swelled to an estimated 2.7 million people at this time. Jesus was the topic of conversation throughout the city. Many who had witnessed Jesus raising Lazarus from the dead were in Jerusalem, and they fueled the intrigue about Christ. As He rode into the city, Jesus immediately attracted a huge crowd. They lined the street and cheered as He passed.

Few people except Jesus probably realized at the time that the Triumphal Entry fulfilled an ancient prophecy that the Messiah would make a victorious ride into Jerusalem on a donkey's colt. (See Zechariah 9:9.) But the people didn't miss the fact that Jesus was the Messiah. At least that is what they thought for a while. But they were expecting a military Messiah who would overthrow the Roman oppression. They wanted a political Messiah who would reestablish their nation.

Jesus deflated the enthusiasm of the crowds and His followers when He made clear and undeniable statements about His imminent death. This news exploded like a bombshell with His fans who still had their adrenaline pumping from the festivities of the Triumphal Entry. All of a sudden, Jesus was no longer the top contender in the Messiah Sweepstakes.

As you read through this passage, try to imagine the range of emotions that the disciples felt. They were as confused about the whole Messiah thing as everyone else. So with the groundswell of support for Jesus at the Triumphal Entry, they must have expected that the time had come for Jesus to assume His rightful role as King. Those disciples must have pictured themselves as key officers in the new administration of Christ's soon-to-be-established Kingdom. They were probably planning how they were going to decorate their palatial offices. But then their hopes were smashed when Jesus said that He was going away.

Jesus knew that news of His impending death left the disciples dazed and discouraged. Like any good coach, Jesus needed to get alone with His "team" and give them one-on-one time with Him so He could make sure they understood the game plan from that point forward. In the next section of John, you'll get to listen in on what Jesus said to His disciples.

Study the Word

1. Read through chapter 9 and describe the way the healed blind man changed his opinion about Jesus. You should be able to find three different impressions of who Christ was and a logical progression among them. (Here's a clue: The more we know about Jesus, the greater He becomes.)

2. Referring to Himself as a shepherd wasn't just a picturesque analogy. The image of a shepherd had great theological significance to the Jews. In fact, it was one more way in which Christ was clearly identifying Himself as God because the Jews often pictured God in this role. But don't take our word for it. Look for the references to God as a shepherd in these verses: Psalm 23:1; 79:13; 95:7; 100:3. (Because most of the Psalms were written by David—who listed "shepherd" on his resume—you won't be surprised to find sheepherder terminology in what he wrote.) In addition, the prophets of Israel also spoke of the coming Messiah as a shepherd. Look at these passages: Isaiah 40:11; Ezekiel 34:12.

3. What is the connection between Christ's power over physical death and His claims regarding the ability to give eternal life?

4. Mary's adoration in John 12 shows us that we worship Jesus not only by attending church, praying, and reading the Bible, but also by the way we live our lives every day. In what practical ways can we show our love for Christ? In what ways might worshiping Jesus be "costly" to you?

5. How could the crowd be so supportive of Jesus at the Triumphal Entry, only to turn against Him in such a short time?

Chapter 7

It is always true that there is no one
closer to men than the man who is
close to God....The nearer we are to
suffering humanity, the nearer
we are to God.

—*William Barclay*

Lessons to Be Learned

We learn some lessons better by seeing them than by listening to a lecture. In John 13, you'll see Jesus acting out the principle of humility. But that isn't the only lesson in the passage. Keep your eye on Judas, and you'll learn about hypocrisy.

HUMILIATION: A Basin and Betrayal

John 13

*Y*ou can unfasten your seatbelt. After a whirlwind tour of the first 12 chapters of John, we're going to slow down the pace a bit. Actually, John himself slows the pace. In chapters 1–12, he covered three years in the life of Christ. In chapters 13–17, he describes what happened at dinner one night.

Just in case you've had a memory lapse from a few pages ago, here is the setup:

- We're in the city of Jerusalem. The city is teeming with residents and visitors who are making preparations for the annual Passover celebration.

- Jesus has publicly announced that He is going to be crucified (12:32).

- Now He gets His disciples away from the crowd so He can give them some encouragement and last-minute instructions.

- Arrangements had been made for Jesus and His 12 disciples to borrow an upstairs room for dinner.

The disciples are still a little clueless as to what is going on. So even though Christ is feeling the stress of the impending events, He focuses on the spiritual welfare of His disciples. As you read through chapters 13–17 of John, look for instances in which Jesus...

- displays His love for His disciples

- forewarns His disciples about what will happen to Him

- forewarns His disciples about what will happen to them

- advises His disciples how to act in His absence

This chapter sets the tone for all that is to follow:

Before the Passover celebration, Jesus knew that his hour had come to leave this world and return to his Father. He now showed the disciples the full extent of his love (13:1).

Jesus did not convey His love in words; He displayed it by His actions. These were the actions of a man who put the concerns of His friends ahead of His own impending crisis. He revealed true servanthood. That's why we have entitled this chapter "Humiliation." He wasn't humiliated by the things that He was about to do. Rather, He was at all times humble throughout the events that followed.

Washing the Disciples' Feet (John 13:1-17)

This story has the humility of Jesus written all over it. After tromping down the dusty streets of Jerusalem all day in sandals, the disciples had dirty feet. Customarily one of the low-ranking household servants washed the feet of the master and his guests. Although the room came equipped with a basin of water and a towel, apparently no servant services were included in the rental contract for the Upper Room.

No one else went for the towel and the basin of water, so Jesus did it. He became the servant. When He finished, Jesus announced that He had just given the disciples an example that He wanted them to follow (13:15). If you are a follower of Christ, consider what this passage teaches about being a servant.

The upstairs room where this all happened is referred to as "the Upper Room." That explains why the teaching that Jesus gave to His disciples in John 13–17 is often referred to as "the Upper Room Discourse." For equally obvious reasons, this entire event is referred to as "the Last Supper."

Jesus saw the need. True servanthood goes beyond doing what you are already required to do. Good servants anticipate what needs to be done, including items that are not in their job description. Sometimes people say, "Helping in that way never occurred to me," but that is usually because they are too busy thinking about themselves. The person with a servant's heart also has a servant's eyes and looks for ways to help others.

Jesus responded with humility. The Son of God assumed the lowly position of a foot washer. Jesus didn't say, "I'm too good for this." He didn't say, "This is not my job." And He didn't give the excuse that a lot of Christians use to avoid an unpleasant task: "I don't have that spiritual gift." A true servant never says, "I'm saving myself for the important stuff." As Jesus demonstrated, any job done in love is important.

Jesus showed no favoritism. Jesus washed everyone's feet. Everyone's. That included Judas, even though Christ knew he was a traitor. The spirit of true servanthood shows love to everyone, not just to those who are lovely.

A Servant *T*akes *A*ction

Luke 22:24 says that during a lull in the conversation at the Last Supper, the disciples started arguing about who was the greatest among them. They ignored the basin of water and the dirty feet. They were too busy boasting about their accomplishments. But Jesus got the job done. While they argued about who should have the most prestigious title, Jesus grabbed the towel. It is not enough to have an intellectual knowledge about the importance of servanthood; you actually have to put your knowledge into action.

In our society, success is pictured by someone who rises above and rules. If we are using Christ as our example, then success is pictured by someone who bends down and serves.

The foot washing by Jesus wasn't just an example of humility and servanthood for the disciples. It also served as symbolism for the spiritual cleansing from sin that each of us needs. When we are saved and our sins are forgiven, we have been spiritually bathed all over. We don't need a full-body wash ever again. But since we keep sinning, a little foot washing (confession) is important so we don't begin to stink. (See John 13:10.)

The Secret Traitor Exposed (John 13:18-30)

Judas is one of the most despicable people in history. But his betrayal becomes all the more shocking when you consider the fact that Judas was sitting right beside Christ during dinner. According to the custom...

- The table was short and U-shaped, and Christ (as the host) sat at the center.

- Low couches were angled around the table so the men could recline on their left side. They leaned on their left elbow with their head by the table, and they ate with their right hand.

Positioned this way, each man had his head near the chest of the man to his left. John—"the disciple whom Jesus loved"—was sitting on the right side of Jesus. This explains the New American Standard version of John 13:25 that says he was "leaning back thus on Jesus' bosom."

When you read 13:18-30, notice that Jesus could talk privately with Judas (and pass the bread to him) without the other disciples noticing. This could have only happened if Judas was sitting immediately to the left of Jesus (since John was on Christ's right side). Here is the amazing thing about that arrangement: In that culture, the place on the left of the host was VIP seating. Here is theologian William Barclay's impression of this situation:

> [Judas] must have been on Jesus's left, so that, just as John's head was in Jesus's breast, Jesus's head was in Judas's. The revealing thing is that *the place on the left of the host was the place of highest honour, kept for the most intimate friend.* When that meal began, Jesus must have said to Judas: "Judas, come and sit beside me tonight; I want specially to talk to you."

Although He knew Judas would betray Him, Christ was gracious and loving toward Judas. This tells us that...

- Judas had every opportunity to abandon his treacherous plan, but he refused to do so.

- Jesus could have exposed Judas to the other disciples, but He refused to do so.

Don't ever think that Jesus was killed by events out of His control. He allowed the traitor to walk out of the room. He permitted the betrayal to proceed. Clearly, Jesus chose to die.

A *New* Commandment? (John 13:31-35)

In John 13:34, Jesus says that He is giving a *new* commandment. But a commandment about loving other people was nothing new. As far back as Moses, God had commanded the Jews to "love your neighbor" (Leviticus 19:18), and as recently as in the Sermon on the Mount, Jesus had told the people to "love your enemies" (Matthew 5:34-35). So what was new about the commandment He gave to the disciples in the Upper Room?

Jesus was emphasizing that the disciples needed to love each other. His teaching wasn't new in the sense of being completely different; rather, it was a fresh approach with a different perspective and emphasis. He told His followers to love each other in the same way that He loved them. This certainly added a new dimension to their understanding of sacrificial love. The disciples might have thought of His recent act of servanthood when He washed their feet. But in about 15 hours or so, they would realize that the full extent of His love for them included His death on the cross.

Loving Each Other?

That "love each other" commandment wasn't limited to the disciples. It applies to all Christians. We are supposed to love each other. The fact that we have been commanded to love suggests that it doesn't come naturally to us. But maybe you already knew that. A little poem makes the point:

> To live above,
> With saints we love,
> Will certainly be glory.
> To live below
> With saints we know,
> Well, that's another story.

The Christian life isn't easy. Jesus knew it wouldn't be so for the disciples, and He wanted them to be committed in love to each other so they could support and encourage each other. And that's exactly how Christians are supposed to treat each other in the twenty-first century.

Peter Speaks When He Should Have Kept His Mouth Shut (John 13:36-38)

As Jesus explains about His death and departure, Peter objects. This is typical Peter behavior. His emotions and hair-trigger responses got him into trouble in the past.

In the ancient Jewish culture, eating with someone at their table was a sign of deep friendship. Doing so was considered a pledge of loyalty. Peter's protestations of loyalty seem a little hollow when you know that he would soon be denying Christ.

Although Christ predicted in John 13:38 that Peter would deny Him (not once, not twice, but three times), Jesus shows no indication of being bitter toward Peter. And aren't you glad—we've probably denied Christ in our own ways more than Peter ever did. And just as Christ loved Peter despite his flaws, He loves us despite ours.

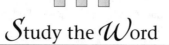

$\mathcal{S}$tudy the $\mathcal{W}$ord

1. When people come to our homes for dinner, we probably don't get out a bucket and wash their feet. What modern-day acts of humility and service might we perform for each other?

2. Jesus loved Judas, His betrayer, to the very end. See how free Jesus was of anger, how uninhibited in His obedience! What happens to us when we hold grudges, harbor resentment, or seek revenge?

3. Our love for other Christians is a useful tool for gauging our spiritual condition. According to 1 John 3:14, what does our love for our brothers and sisters show us? According to John 13:35, who will notice our love for each other, and what will it show them? How do Romans 12:9-10 and Philippians 2:1-4 deepen your understanding of what loving each other means?

4. Peter's confession was bold in the Upper Room, but it evaporated under the heat of testing. What is the difference between bravado and bravery, between just being loud and truly being loyal?

5. Jesus wasn't primarily interested in cleaning the dirt off the disciples' feet. What was His main concern?

Chapter 8

He expressed a wish that I should read to
him: and when I asked, "From what book?"
he said, "Need you ask? There is but one."
So I chose the fourteenth chapter of St.
John. And after listening with devotion he
said, "Well, this is a great comfort."

—*J.G. Lockhart,* from *Life of Sir Walter Scott*

*W*ords to *R*emember

Have you ever wondered what the head coach says to the team in the locker room before the start of the Super Bowl? Or, if you are more into hoops, what the coach says to the team before the start of the seventh game of the NBA finals? We suspect that speeches in those situations are intended to calm frazzled nerves and inspire confidence. They may include a reminder about putting aside distractions and focusing on the fundamentals. Strategies for dealing with what's ahead will be reviewed one last time.

Keep those images in mind as you read this next chapter. You'll find yourself in an "Upper Room" instead of a locker room, but you'll be listening in on the greatest team leader of all time as He gives a pep talk to His guys before the biggest event in the history of the world.

SUMMATION: Famous Last Words

John 14–16

*O*ften when people are dying, they place great significance on their final words. (Bruce is a probate lawyer, so you can take his word for it.) They know their time is short, so they talk about those things that are the most important.

Jesus wasn't any different. He didn't want the disciples to be disillusioned by His death. He wanted them to know it was part of God's master plan. So in the last moments with His disciples, He told them positive things about the future so their faith in the certainty of God's plan would be strengthened as those things occurred:

> *I have told you these things before they happen so that you will believe when they do happen* (John 14:29).

And He told them about some of the hardships of the future so they would be prepared in advance and wouldn't give up:

> *I have told you these things so that you won't fall away* (John 16:1).

As you read this passage, you can sense that Christ is comforting, motivating, and instructing His disciples—all at the same time. Along the way, Christ delivers a message that is relevant for Christians of every generation.

Returning to the Father (John 14:1-14)

When Jesus said that He was returning to His Father's house, He was referring to heaven (14:2). To keep the disciples from fearing that they would be separated from Him forever, He quickly added that heaven was their eternal destination, too (14:3). And, of course, they knew how to get there (14:4). "Wait a minute," shouts Thomas. "We don't know how to get there." And in response to Thomas, Christ enunciates with undeniable clarity that belief in Him is the only way of salvation:

I am the way, the truth, and the life. No one can come to the Father except through me (John14:6).

This passage ends with two curious verses:

We will do greater works than Jesus did (14:12). Is it possible for mere humans to outperform Christ? Well, yes, in a sense. First of all, we aren't mere humans when we are empowered by the Holy Spirit (more about that in a few pages). And let's not forget that Christ's ministry was limited to the regions of Palestine. Within a few decades after His death, His followers had taken the Gospel message throughout the known world. In that sense, at least, His disciples did more than Christ did.

He will do anything that we ask in His name (14:13). Really? Anything? Yes, but notice the qualifier. We are not promised to get anything we ask for. We are only promised to get what we ask for in Christ's name. That means more than tacking on an "in Jesus' name I pray" tag line at the end of your prayer. It means praying unselfishly in line with God's desires and plan. Our prayers always need to be qualified within the parameters of God's will. In that context then, prayers for the accomplishment of His will shall be granted.

---

*W*as the *L*ast *S*upper a *P*assover *M*eal?

Mark 14:12-16 and Luke 22:7 state that Jesus and the disciples celebrated the Passover meal at the Last Supper. Traditionally the Passover meal was held on Friday evening. People who try to find discrepancies in the Bible have pointed out that (1) John never refers to the Last Supper as the Passover meal, and (2) several verses in John indicate the Last Supper was held on Wednesday night. Does this mean that the Bible is inconsistent, contradictory, or unreliable?

While John does not ever clearly say that the Last Supper was the Passover meal, he gives descriptions that make that fact clear. For example, John 13:23 says that the disciples and Jesus *reclined* as they ate. It was common for people in ancient cultures to recline on little couches at mealtime. But Jews only did this at Passover time; the rest of the time they honored the invention of the chair.

While John suggests that the Last Supper occurred on Wednesday night, nothing in Mark or Luke says the Passover meal was celebrated by Jesus and the disciples on Friday. Some scholars believe that Jesus arranged with His disciples to celebrate the Passover meal one day early. That is a prerogative that Jesus could have taken. (He never was one to be confined by man-made traditions that didn't make sense.)

Promise of the Holy Spirit (John 14:15-31)

At this point in His teaching, Christ reveals the Person who will continue teaching the disciples. They weren't going to be spiritually abandoned; God would send the Holy Spirit to live inside them.

The Greek word that is used for "Holy Spirit" is *parakletos*. The English language has no precise translation of *parakletos*, but the general meaning is conveyed by these words and names:

- the Comforter

- the Counselor

- the Helper

- the one who comes alongside

That is exactly what the disciples were going to need: God's Spirit to direct and guide them.

The Vine and the Branches (John 15:1-8)

We both live in Fresno, California. If our Chamber of Commerce is doing its job, you might know that Fresno is the raisin capital of the world. As you would expect, there are lots of vineyards in our vicinity, so we know a bit about vines. (We aren't farmers, but we talk to people who are.)

Jesus said that He is the vine and we are the branches. God, as the gardener, has to prune the vine so that it will grow stronger and produce more fruit. That's exactly what the farmers do in Fresno. We've seen it. In January the pruning begins. Dead branches are cut off and discarded. The healthy branches are pruned and trimmed and tied to increase the growth potential.

It doesn't take a grape grower to understand the analogy: God is going to chop off the dead branches. That would include the Jews who failed to acknowledge Christ as the Messiah, as well as everyone today who refuses to believe in Christ.

The four Gospels report three instances in which Jesus taught at great length. Matthew 5–7 contains "the Sermon on the Mount," where Jesus taught about the kingdom of heaven. The Olivet Discourse, in which Christ describes end-of-the-world events, is reported in Matthew 24–25, Mark 13, and Luke 21. And the third is the Upper Room Discourse of John 13–17.

God prunes the healthy branches. Even if you are a productive and fruitful Christian, you can expect a little pruning in your life (and not just in January). We've all got some rough edges that need to be trimmed. We need to be trained to grow God's way and not our own way. The pruning process isn't pleasant, but it results in more spiritual fruitfulness in our lives. (By the way, if you are interested in knowing what spiritual fruit looks like, see Galatians 5:22-23.)

Love Each Other! That's a Command! (John 15:9-17)

Isn't Christ's command to His disciples to love each other interesting? We often think that love is an emotion, that you can't control it, and that you either have it for someone or you don't. But love is evidently not a fickle sensation if Christ commands us to affirmatively do it. Here's the difference: People sometimes use the word *love* as a noun. They erroneously equate it as a thing that you either possess or lack, as in "I don't have any love for him."

But *love* isn't a noun in this context. It is a verb. It is something you do, as in "Jesus loved the disciples by washing their feet."

When *love* is a verb, you can follow Christ's command to love each other even if you don't feel like it.

You Won't Win a Popularity Contest (John 15:18–16:4)

Jesus had been giving His disciples lots of good news, but now it is time for the bad news. As He shifts from talking about love, He tells them that their faith in Him will make them unpopular with the world's culture. As a result, they can expect to be...

- hated

- arrested

- beaten

- killed

If you had been in Christ's place, trying to recruit followers, would you have mentioned the severe downsides? Jesus didn't pull any punches. He laid it on the line. He told His disciples that the road of faith is not easy. Risk and danger are involved. And the same is true today. In some areas, Christians are criticized for their faith; in other parts of the world, Christians are killed for the faith. Following the Lord includes more than just serenely worshiping at church. If we are doing our job as Christians, we will be out in the world—a world that is hostile toward Christ.

The Ministry of the Holy Spirit (John 16:5-15)

Imagine the emotions surging through the disciples as they listened to all that Jesus was saying. They must have wondered if they were going to be able to handle the assignment Jesus was giving them. Of course, Jesus knew that they, in their own strength, were woefully incapable of doing much of anything. So He summarizes the role of the Holy Spirit to make clear to the disciples that they need to look to God's power instead of their own inabilities.

At the time John was writing his Gospel at the end of the first century A.D., the Christian church was under persecution by the Roman government. Christianity was illegal. Merely identifying yourself as a Christian could be grounds for the death penalty.

Often Christians assume bringing their friends to the point of believing in Jesus Christ is their personal duty and responsibility. They feel that unless they take whatever measures are necessary to guarantee a conversion experience, they have failed as witnesses for Christ. Such a viewpoint is inconsistent with Christ's teaching in this passage. The Holy Spirit's ministry includes...

- convincing people of their sin

- convincing the world of God's righteousness

- convincing the world of judgment

We aren't under any pressure to wring a confession out of anyone. Our job is to present the Gospel; the Holy Spirit's job is to convince each person of his or her need for a Savior.

But the Holy Spirit's job doesn't stop there. Jesus also explained that the Holy Spirit is the Spirit of Truth (16:13). The Spirit of Truth guides us in our understanding of Scripture and gives us assurance of our salvation. But you can't get by with just a brief encounter with the Spirit of Truth. You don't get spiritual understanding all in one shot, but rather through a continual process. That's why Jesus said that the Spirit of Truth will be our guide. On a daily basis, for the rest of our lives, the Holy Spirit is available to us.

Sadness Out, Joy In (John 16:16-33)

Jesus brings His teaching to a close by giving His disciples a long-term perspective. Although they couldn't figure it out at the time, John had made sense of it by the time he wrote the Gospel about 50 or 60 years later. Jesus explained that the Christian life is more than just our existence here on earth. He was leaving the disciples, but they will be reunited later when Christ establishes His kingdom at the end of the current age. When viewed from this eternal perspective...

- Sorrow turns to joy. No matter how bad things get on earth for the Christian, the future holds the promise of the joy of heaven.

- The eternal joy of heaven can never be taken away. Any present pain will be quickly forgotten when we realize our future joy.

- Our joy doesn't have to be postponed. Even though our present circumstances may be difficult, we can experience a sense of joy right now when we realize that God loves each of us and is in charge of all that happens to us.

Joy can come from our relationship with God. Jesus paid the penalty for our sins on the cross, so we have direct access to God Almighty. We have the freedom to ask anything from Him, and God will grant those requests if they are in the best interests of the kingdom. And nobody knows what's best better than God Himself.

When you understand Christ's perspective, His closing line makes perfect sense. His Crucifixion was all part of God's master plan. That was the greatest word of encouragement He could give to the disciples. They needed to know that when difficulties came their way, God was still in charge.

> *I have told you all this so that you may have peace in me. Here on earth you will have many trials and sorrows. But take heart, because I have overcome the world* (John 16:33).

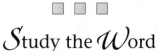

Study the Word

1. In what way would Jesus' teaching on heaven comfort the disciples (John 14:1-14)? How does a "heavenly mind-set" help us today?

2. Read John 14:15-31 again. Identify the things that the Holy Spirit will do. Describe the relationship between love and obedience. Explain the value of the gift given by Christ to His disciples.

3. What is the key to bearing fruit (John 15:1-8)? How do we do that?

4. Read John 15:9-17 and count the number of times Christ uses the word *love*. Each time you see that word, determine if it is being used as a noun or a verb. Is Christ describing an emotion or an action?

5. Do you think Christians suffer persecution in our culture? Do you think the world really "hates" Christians (John 15:18–16:4)? Give examples to support your answer.

6. In John 16:5-15, we see that Jesus is confident that His work will continue because of the Holy Spirit. What can we be confident about because of the Holy Spirit?

7. In John 16:16-33, Jesus says that the disciples will experience sadness and joy, trials and peace. Why will they be sad? What reasons will they have to rejoice? What trials will they have? How can they have peace? Is your situation similar to theirs?

Chapter 9

Christ's work was the impartation of life. His
teachings, His signs, His person, His death
and resurrection were all parts of His calling.
The prayer [John 17] that He offered is, in a
sense, a report of His fulfillment of His com-
mission before returning to the Father.

—*Merrill C. Tenney*

$\mathcal{T}$ime to $\mathcal{P}$ray

You are about to read what is often called Christ's "high priestly prayer." It is Christ's prayer for His disciples. This will be His last few moments with them before the events of His arrest and Crucifixion. With time so precious, Jesus makes the best use of it. He talks with His Father.

BENEDICTION: A Closing Prayer

John 17

The time with the disciples in the Upper Room ends with a prayer. If we knew that we were about to be nailed to a cross, our prayers might be on the selfish side. But Jesus was never selfish before, and His prayer isn't really about Him as much as it is about other people.

One thing comes across loud and clear in this prayer. Forces of evil are at work in the world. Jesus' perspective is not surprising because the forces of Satan at that very moment were overseeing the betrayal by Judas and preparations for the Crucifixion of Christ.

Christ's prayer can be dissected into three sections. In the beginning, He prays for Himself, then He prays specifically for His disciples, and then He prays for future believers who will respond to the disciples' message. Jesus appears to have prayed this prayer while He and the disciples (except Judas) sat around the table in the Upper Room. The disciples must have been encouraged to hear Jesus pray about them. You will be encouraged when you read Christ's prayer for you.

The Hour Has Come (The Middle of the Bible)

We interrupt this chapter to give you an interesting bit of Bible trivia: You are now at the exact middle of the Bible. We suspect that you are skeptical because you notice that your open Bible has many more pages on the left side than on the right side, so let us explain.

We can calculate the middle of the Bible in several ways:

- *Page Count:* We can take the total number of pages and then divide by two. In most Bibles, that would put us somewhere in the Old Testament, perhaps near Psalm 130. (If footnotes take up space on every page in your Bible, then the "page counting" calculation won't be precise.)

- *Verse Count:* You can count all of the verses in the Bible and then divide by two. We'll save you the trouble. The Bible contains 31,173 verses. The middle verse is Psalm 118:8.

- *Between the Sections:* Many people consider that blank page between the end of the Old Testament (the last verse in the last chapter of Malachi) and the first page of the New Testament (Matthew 1:1) to be the middle of the Bible.

When calculating the halfway point, we prefer to use the perspective of the writers. Think about this:

- The entire Old Testament looks forward in time to the Messiah's work of salvation. As early as Genesis 3, God referred to the time when evil would be conquered. And God made a promise to Abraham that through his descendants, all of the people of the earth would be blessed. The symbolism grew stronger through the time of Moses. Some of the psalms and many of the writings of the major and minor prophets refer to the work of the Messiah and humanity's salvation through Him. The Person and work of the Messiah is a theme that is woven deeply into the Old Testament.

- The Gospels show that during the life of Christ, the question of the day was, Is Jesus the Messiah that everyone is awaiting?

- After the Crucifixion and Resurrection, the evidence was clear (at least to anyone who was objective about it) that Jesus truly was the Son of God and the promised Messiah. From that point on, the focus of the New Testament shifts to Christ's return. He said that He was coming back, and that's what people have been waiting for since. That expectation is preached in the book of Acts, and it is the hope that Paul and the other epistle writers emphasized as they encouraged those early Christians who suffered persecution. It is the focal point of the future prophecies of the book of Revelation.

So, we see the middle of the Bible as the work of Christ on the cross. The Old Testament and part of each of the Gospels *look forward* to the Cross. The rest of the Bible *looks back* at the Cross as the basis for *looking forward* to Christ's return. Thus, the Cross is the center point of the Bible.

God had a timetable for Christ's work of salvation of the Cross. Earlier in His ministry, Jesus declared that the timing was not right, usually with a statement to the effect that the "hour" of His suffering had "not yet come." (See John 2:4; 7:6-8,30; 8:20.) But with the gathering of the disciples in that upper room, Jesus knew that the time was now. This was the prelude to the Crucifixion, and Jesus knew it. (Go back and read John 13:1.)

So it is not surprising that at the outset of His prayer in John 17:1, Jesus declares that "the time has come." Jesus knew that He was entering into the time of the cross. This was it...the focal point of not only the Bible, but of all human history.

Christ's Prayer for Himself (John 17:1-5)

Jesus asked that God the Father would glorify Him. At first glance, that prayer may seem selfish. But study this passage closely. Jesus was asking that He be glorified in the impending events so that glory would reflect back on God the Father. He wanted to be a conduit for people's attention that would direct praise and worship to His Father. The glory that Jesus sought was in the fulfillment of what His Father had sent Him to earth to do.

Christ's prayer is an example for us to follow. We shouldn't pray for our own selfish wants and desires. Our prayer should always be that we accomplish God's will. The focus of our prayers should be what Christ wants, not what we want. We shouldn't be praying to convince God to move over to our way of thinking. Instead, our prayers should align our desires with what God wants to accomplish.

In this passage you'll come across the words *glory* and *glorify* quite a few times. A little explanation might be helpful because *glorify* probably isn't part of your daily vocabulary. In John's day, *glory* applied not only to something's appearance but also to the accomplishment of its purpose (as when a field of wheat came into its glory when it was ready for harvest). In this passage, Christ's glorification refers to His accomplishment of the task of bringing God's plan of salvation to the world through His impending death on the cross.

But the glorification that is referred to in this passage isn't limited to Jesus completion of God's plan of salvation. It includes these additional aspects:

- Christ glorified (honored) His Father by being obedient to His Father's plan.

- Christ was to be glorified through the Resurrection, which would follow the Crucifixion. He would triumph over the worst that evil could do to Him.

- The Crucifixion was the threshold that Jesus had to pass before He could return to heaven and the glorious presence of His Father.

- Christ and His heavenly Father would soon be glorified by those who would believe on Christ as their Savior.

So the imminent Crucifixion would mean Christ's glorification in the cross (17:1,4), His glorification in heaven (17:5) and His glorification in the church (17:2,3,10).

*E*ternal *L*ife

Don't miss the definition of eternal life in 17:3. Some people think that eternal life means living forever. Well, that's a part of it. But the real benefit of eternal life is knowing God and being in fellowship with Jesus Christ. It is all about having an intimate knowledge of God and a personal relationship with Him. That is what's going to make living forever so wonderful. You can spend forever in a close relationship with the almighty God of the universe.

Christ's Prayer for His Disciples (John17:6-19)

Luke 6:12 says that Jesus prayed all night before He chose His 12 disciples. Because He prayed for them at the beginning, His prayer for them at the end comes as no surprise.

This portion of Christ's prayer addresses the evil in the world that will oppose the ministry of the disciples. Jesus prayed for their safety in the midst of hostile surroundings. He prayed that they would be made pure by God's truth. Interestingly, Jesus didn't pray that God would remove or insulate the disciples from the evil in the world. He knew that they had to be in the world to be effective ministers of the Gospel. He just wanted them protected so that they didn't become enveloped by the culture. That's the significant difference. If we are to be effective disciples for Christ, we need to be *in* the world but not *of* the world. (See Romans 12:2.)

A secondary emphasis in Christ's prayer for His disciples crops up in verses 11-19. He prayed that they would have the proper relationship to each other and to the unbelieving world:

- ***Disciples' Relationship with Each Other:*** Christ wanted His disciples to be united as one (17:11). Jesus desired that His followers be connected to each other in the same closeness that Christ shared with His Father. In the same way that the Father, the Son, and the Holy Spirit have different roles but are bonded together as One, Christ wanted the disciples to share a sense of oneness. Such unity would bring glory to God, and it would serve to keep the disciples strong in the midst of the adversity they would face.

- ***Disciples' Relationship with Unbelievers:*** In verses 14-19, Christ's prayer reveals how He wanted the disciples to relate to the unbelieving world. (By the way, the principles of Christ's prayer apply to us as well.) He didn't want them to be judgmental and arrogant, and He didn't want them to separate themselves from the world around them. That was the approach of the Pharisees, and it was anything but winsome. Instead, He wanted His disciples to have a sense of mission or purpose about their role in the world. It is a role of bringing God's truth to those who do not yet believe. (See 17:18.)

Christ's Prayer for You (John 17:20-26)

I am praying not only for these disciples but also for all who will ever believe in me because of their testimony (John 17:20).

Jesus was talking about you. The emphasis of His prayer for you is on unity. He wants you to live in unity with the heavenly Father. And He wants you to live in harmony with other believers.

Don't miss the emphasis on intimacy. Christ wants you to be in a close, intimate relationship with other believers. How personal? Well, He wants your fellowship with other Christians to be as close as His relationship with His Heavenly Father. (See 17:21.) This kind of unity doesn't come naturally. What seems to come naturally between Christians are things like gossip and petty arguments. But such behavior only divides Christians. Jesus wanted the opposite result. He wants us to be bonded to each other. We have to work at the kind of relationship He wants us to have with each other. It is a two-step process. First, we need to commit ourselves to loving God and being obedient to His commands. Then, we need to show love to other Christians.

The benefit of being in right relationships with other Christians is not only for us. Our love for each other attracts unbelievers to Christ. Jesus explained this principle to the disciples in John 13:35 when He said that the world will know that we are His disciples if we love each other. When the love of God is in us, the world can't help but notice.

Finally, don't miss what may be the best part of Christ's prayer for you. Notice in verse 24 that Jesus is anxious for you to be with Him. Jesus wants all believers to be with Him where He is so that they can see His glory. That verse refers not only to the disciples but also to you. Make this verse your hope for the future. No matter how tough your circumstances are here on earth, Christ is anxious to welcome you to heaven, where you can directly experience His glory.

Jesus prayed for you then, and He is still praying for you now. (See Romans 8:34 and Hebrews 7:25.)

■ ■ ■

$\mathcal{S}$tudy the $\mathcal{W}$ord

1. Read about Christ's prayer in the Garden of Gethsemane after He left the Upper Room. (Matthew 26:36-46; Mark 14:32-42; Luke 22:39-46.) These passages will give you a better perspective on the agony that Christ was enduring as the Crucifixion drew near. What additional insights are provided by each of these passages?

2. To reinforce the principles that Christ taught in chapters 14–17, read them again. As you read, make a note of...

    • the things God does for us

    • the things God gives to us

3. Remembering what God does for us and gives to us, the disciples could endure the days ahead with a present joy and a future hope. Have God's presence and power helped you endure difficult circumstances in the past?

4. Read Philippians 2:9-11. Explain how Christ's death on the cross brought glory to Him.

5. Review what Christ prayed for His disciples and for you. Now describe the role that Christ wants you to play in the lives of other Christians. What is your role in the life of unbelievers?

Chapter 10

Our suffering is not worthy of the name
of suffering. When I consider my crosses,
tribulations, and temptations, I shame
myself almost to death, thinking what
they are in comparison of the sufferings
of my blessed Savior Christ Jesus.

—*Martin Luther*

Read It Again
for the First Time

Do you have a few movies that you've seen so often that you can quote the punch lines and some of the dialogue by heart? The story is so good that you never get tired of hearing it. The next four chapters of John tell a true-life story that never gets old. If it were just a clinical recitation of an impersonal, irrelevant bit of history, it would be boring even the first time you heard it. But John 18–21 tells a story of horror and heroics, of tragedy and triumph, of larceny and love. And best of all, you are at the center of the story because *you* were the motivation for what Christ did.

As you read the next four chapters, try to imagine how the disciples felt as the events unfolded. After all, you already know the outcome, but the disciples never had a clue about what was going to happen next. They were surprised each step of the way. We think you'll get a sense of the surprise the disciples felt. Nobody knows how those disciples felt better than John.

PROSECUTION: **Arrested, Tried, and Convicted**

John 18:1–19:16

*W*hat's *A*head

- ☐ No Ordinary Group of Admirers (John 18:1-11)

- ☐ Trial of Messiahship in the Council Chambers (John 18:12-27)

- ☐ Trial of Guilt in the Courtroom (John 18:28–19:16)

*M*any artists have drawn beautiful portraits of Christ. But we think some miss the mark. We aren't big fans of those pictures that make Christ look pale and emaciated, soft and fragile. Yes, Christ had a tender side to Him, but He was a rugged guy. After all, those rough fishermen wouldn't have been the disciples of an effeminate leader. Christ is a man's man, and nowhere is this better illustrated than in John 18.

This chapter finds us in a garden on a hillside outside of the city of Jerusalem. Jesus went to this place on many occasions to find peace and solitude. But He wasn't expecting to find tranquility there this night. He knew that what awaited Him was Judas and a mob.

No Ordinary Group of Admirers (John 18:1-11)

The group that confronted Jesus in the garden was not the usual crowd that customarily greeted Him. No admirers in this group. They were all hostile toward Him. The chief priests and elders put together this group of...

- some chief priests and some elders (lay leaders) of the Sanhedrin

- some Pharisees

- Temple police

- a contingent of Roman soldiers

This mob was armed and dangerous. They came storming into the garden carrying torches, lanterns, and clubs. The soldiers had their spears and swords. Think of this as the mob scene from *Beauty and the Beast*, but this was no cartoon or fairy tale. The mob mentality was very real and very dangerous.

- *They were vigilantes.* With a perverted view of justice, they took the law into their own hands.

- *They were mindless.* Most of them were acting irrationally in response to the directions of a few leaders with evil motives.

- *They were cowards.* They acted at night so the public wouldn't know what was going on.

Perhaps as many as 1000 men came to arrest Jesus and 11 of His disciples. Those were odds of 99 to 1. But you can understand why. On several previous occasions they had tried to arrest Jesus, but He had escaped and vanished before they could do it. (See Luke 4:28-30; John 7:32-34,44-46.)

Jesus and the disciples were essentially unarmed. According to Luke 22:38, the disciples only carried two swords among them.

Judas, How Could You?

Apparently the Jewish leaders had planned to arrest Jesus after the Passover (when many of His supporters would have left Jerusalem and gone back to their home-towns). But according to Matthew 26:14-16, Judas approached the chief priests and volunteered to turn Jesus over to them. He demanded a finder's fee of 30 pieces of silver (about the price of a slave). How could Judas have been a disciple of Christ for approximately three years and then betray Him?

Although Judas joined up as a disciple, he apparently wasn't attracted to Jesus by His teachings or His character. Judas believed that Jesus was the Messiah, but like the other disciples, he assumed that Jesus was going to establish His kingdom in a political sense rather than in a spiritual sense. Judas believed that money and power were going to be swirling around the Messiah, and Judas wanted a piece of the action. But when Jesus started talking about dying, and when He refused to lead the crowds at the Triumphal Entry in a political revolt, Judas saw the handwriting on the wall. He knew he better cut the best deal he could while he was still in a position to make a buck.

For the pathetic end of the Judas story, read Matthew 27:1-10.

Why Wasn't John More Critical of Judas?

Maybe John understood God's love and our sin. Jesus showed love to Judas the entire time. If Jesus could love him, John and the other disciples shouldn't be unfairly critical of him. Or maybe John recognized his own sin. Each and every sin is rebellion against God. Judas betrayed Jesus, but we do the same thing when we intentionally sin in utter rejection of Christ's love.

Why Did the Jewish Leaders Want Jesus Killed?

The Jewish leaders could articulate a long list of grievances against Christ. According to them...

- He broke the rules of the Torah.

- He claimed to have authority equal to God.

- He broke social customs and fraternized with social outcasts (and said that God relates to people in the same way).

- He said that God's grace extends to those outside the Torah (to people who didn't devote themselves to religion).

- He challenged the authority of the Pharisees and even corrected their interpretation (though He was uneducated and came from a poor background).

Of course, all of the things that Jesus said and did were acceptable to God and in accordance with God's principles, but they violated the man-made regulations and interpretations that the Pharisees had instituted for their own benefit.

These were the official reasons that the religious leaders gave for arresting Christ. But those weren't the real reasons they were out to get Him. In reality, He was a threat to their power and challenged the hypocrisy of their lifestyle. Because He could perform miracles and had great crowd appeal, He was all the more dangerous. He had to be stopped "for the good of society." And not just any form of death would do. He had to be crucified because that is the worst type of execution, reserved for the worst people. If the religious leaders couldn't discredit the way Jesus lived, they would try to discredit Him in the eyes of the people by the way He died.

Lend Me Your Ear

Peter came to the defense of Christ. He whipped out his sword and cut off the ear of the servant of the High Priest. Don't be impressed with Peter's aim. He wasn't trying to slice the ear from the head. He was probably trying to crack a few skulls. He was just a bad shot; he missed the target. (You might say it was an ear miss.)

But Jesus immediately told Peter to put the sword back into the sheath. From this account and from Matthew 26:47-56, you can find three reasons why Jesus told Peter to put his sword away:

1. Peter's action was *dangerous*. Violence begets more violence. In any clash of sabers, the disciples were sure to be the losers. Jesus didn't want physical aggression to break out. His concern was for the safety of His disciples. (See John 18:8.)

2. The show of strength was *needless*. Jesus didn't need Peter to defend Him. God could have sent down thousands of angels to do the job. And we guess that guardian angels are more accurate with their swords than Peter was with his. (See Matthew 26:53.)

3. The rescue attempt was *pointless*. Jesus didn't want to be defended. He didn't want to interrupt the progression of events that would take Him to the cross. Crucifixion was in God's plan—it was "the cup" which the Father had given Him to drink—and He wanted to get on with it. (See John 18:11.)

Trial of Messiahship in the Council Chambers (John 18:12-27)

The arrest of Christ happened between 11:00 P.M. and 1:00 A.M. As soon as Christ was taken into custody, the disciples fled. (See Matthew 26:56.) We don't see any sign of the disciples until Peter pokes into the courtyard.

Have you ever wondered why these official proceedings were conducted in the middle of the night? The timing was more than strange—it was illegal. But that didn't stop the religious leaders who were supposedly so concerned about adhering to the strict letter of the law.

Although John only reports two of them, Jesus actually had three separate hearings before Jewish authorities:

The First Jewish Hearing

The Jewish authorities began with a preliminary hearing before Annas (John 18:12-24). Annas was formerly the High Priest. That was a position of power, and the benefits extended for a lifetime even though the term of office may have only been a few years. Historians reveal that Annas was one of the most corrupt High Priests. He siphoned personal wealth out of the Temple by cheating the worshipers (just as the money changers that Jesus drove out of the Temple courtyard did). Annas treated the Temple as a family business. After his term as Chief Priest ended, his sons got the job. Then it was given to his son-in-law, Caiaphas. Annas played a large part in the arrest and phony conviction of Jesus because He was a threat to Annas' scheme of revenue raising. This was Annas' chance for payback.

The Second Jewish Hearing

After the encounter with Annas, Temple guards hauled Jesus over to the council chambers of Caiaphas. (In 18:13,24, John refers to him as the High Priest.) This trial occurred in the middle of the night.

The Third Jewish Hearing

Matthew 27:1-2 reports that early in the morning the council convened for a third session. Here the Jewish leaders confirmed and approved the sham hearings before Annas and Caiaphas. They decided to put Jesus to death. Although they found Jesus guilty of technicalities, they overlooked the illegalities of the proceedings:

- arrest without an indictment

- questioning someone in an attempt to obtain self-incrimination

- convening judicial proceedings of this type in the evening

- holding a proceeding that involved a death sentence in the council chambers rather than the Temple

- holding a hearing that involved capital punishment in private

- testimony that did not include specifics of date, time, and place

- pronouncing the guilty verdict without polling the members of the council

- not having scribes tabulate the council's votes

Test of Discipleship in the Courtyard

During the proceedings in the council chambers, Peter was standing in the courtyard. In John 18:15-18, John tells the story of Peter's three-time denial of Christ.

Just as Christ had predicted in the Upper Room, a rooster crowed after Peter's third denial. That sound must have felt like a dagger in Peter's heart as he realized his failure as a disciple of Christ. Boasting of loyalty in the safety of the Upper Room was easy. But Peter's loyalty evaporated when it really mattered.

Some scholars interpret "the rooster crowed" to mean something other than the obvious. A "no roosters allowed" law applied to the inner city of Jerusalem. And 3:00 A.M. might have been a little early for a rooster to be crowing. But the Roman military troops had a changing of the guard every three hours during the night (at 6:00 P.M., 9:00 P.M., 12:00 A.M., 3:00 A.M., and 6:00 A.M.). The 3:00 A.M. shift was announced with the blaring of a trumpet. It was referred to as a "cock-crow," and everybody in

Jerusalem knew about it (probably because it woke them up). Perhaps this is what Jesus was referring to. Whether it was a rooster or a trumpet, it happened after the third denial, and Peter knew exactly what it meant.

Trial of Guilt in the Courtroom
(John 18:28–19:16)

Although the Jewish leaders declared a death sentence, they didn't have the power to carry out that penalty. The Roman authorities had taken away that power. Clearly, Jesus' death required a Roman sentence.

Just as Jesus had three hearings before the Jewish authorities, He also had three separate hearings before Roman officials.

The First Roman Hearing

The Jews first took Jesus to Pilate, the Roman governor. They presented charges of treason and rebellion against Him. (Of course, these were the crimes that the Jews found Him guilty of, but they had to re-characterize the charges so they would qualify for the death sentence under Roman law.) After questioning Christ, Pilate determined that He was innocent. However, Pilate didn't dismiss the charges because he feared that the Jews would report to Caesar that a rebel had been released.

The Second Roman Hearing

So Pilate punted and sent Jesus to Herod Agrippa, a higher-ranking Roman authority who happened to be in Jerusalem to monitor the activities of the Jews during Passover. Herod thought he might get to see a few miracles from Jesus, but Christ wasn't in the mood to satisfy

Herod's insincere curiosity. Herod grew impatient and sent Jesus back to Pilate. (See Luke 23:6-12.)

The Third Roman Hearing

Pilate didn't want to convict Jesus, but he didn't want to infuriate the Jewish leaders either. He suggested a few compromises: He suggested letting Jesus off with a good beating and whipping, and he suggested that Jesus be released under the annual tradition of pardoning one prisoner. But the Jewish authorities would accept nothing less than a death sentence (and they requested the release of a known terrorist, Barabbas, instead of Christ). Pilate wimped out and gave them what they wanted instead of following his personal impression of Christ's innocence. John 19:16 is a sad commentary on Pilate's lack of character: "Then Pilate gave Jesus to them to be crucified."

■ ■ ■

$\mathcal{S}$tudy the $\mathcal{W}$ord

1. Imagine having a huge mob of armed vigilantes coming after you in the middle of the night. What emotions does Jesus seem to have in John 18:1-11?

2. Peter tried to help Jesus in 18:10-11. Explain how three people tried to help God—and just made matters worse. Then summarize God's word to Jehoshaphat.

   • Abraham (Genesis 16:1-2)

   • Joseph (Genesis 37:5-11)

   • Moses (Exodus 2:11-15)

   • Jehoshaphat (2 Chronicles 20:13-17)

3. What did Jesus do to try to save Himself during the Jewish and Roman trials?

4. How could Peter's pride in the Upper Room turn into such timidity in 18:15-18,25-27? What do you think can help us remain courageous and loyal when we're put to the test?

5. What does Pilate's response reveal about the Jewish leaders' intentions?

Chapter 11

That is true worship—a recognition that Jesus is God, and that God has submitted Himself to death on our behalf! And true worship leads us to action, to service, to obedience. When our hearts are filled with true worship, when our hands are engaged in true service, we are united with the one who made the entire universe, the one who is the great "I am." That is a thrilling, exalting thought. And that is the message of the Gospel of John.

—Ray C. Stedman

Not a Pretty Picture

Somewhere along the line, we have lost the horror of the Crucifixion scene. Maybe we don't want to frighten the little children in the Easter pageants at church. But the scene was gruesome and frightening, and we trivialize the suffering of Christ when we forget that fact.

CRUCIFIXION: **Beaten, Dead, and Buried**

John 19:17-42

*I*f you had to pick one series of events in the life of Christ as most important, you would probably choose those that began with the Crucifixion and ended with the Resurrection. In fact, those events are the most important events in the history of the world (at least if eternal salvation is important to you). That the cross has become an important symbol of Christianity is no surprise. But the symbolism may be more significant than you realize.

The Cross as a Symbol of Suffering

The physical suffering that Christ endured on the cross was horrible. But it didn't begin at the cross—it started much earlier in the morning, shortly after He was arrested. Think of the brutality that He suffered:

- The Roman soldiers whipped Him. These whips had braided leather thongs with sharp pieces of metal at the end of every strand. The flogging shredded the skin and back muscles of Christ.

- Soldiers fashioned a wreath of thorn branches into a mock crown and jammed it down on His skull. The thorns themselves were an inch long.

- Soldiers also slugged and beat Him.

After the physical abuse that He suffered, He was forced to carry His own cross partway through the city. Whether He carried only the cross member (which would have weighed about 75 pounds) or was forced to drag the entire cross (weighing about 300 pounds) is not clear.

The Romans tied many criminals to the cross, but they drove seven-inch-long nails through Jesus' hands and feet.

The suffering of Christ was neither quick nor easy. It was drawn out and painful. He died on the cross at about 3:00 P.M. from a combination of shock, asphyxia, and blood loss. Whenever you think of the cross, think of His suffering.

The Cross as a Symbol of Sacrifice

Since the time of Abraham, God had required a blood sacrifice for sin. Until the arrival of the Messiah, God's people sacrificed representative animals on altars in the Tabernacle or Temple. But everyone knew that these were only temporary.

The penalty for sin is death. (See Romans 3:23.) We all deserve that penalty, but Jesus paid it when He died on the cross. He was the real-life sacrifice that was offered on

> Amazing love! How can it be that thou, my God, shouldst die for me?
>
> —*Charles Wesley*

the cross. Thus, the cross itself is the representation of the sacrifice that Christ made for us.

The Cross as a Symbol of Scandal

The Jewish leaders insisted on crucifixion as the manner for Christ's death (John 19:6,15). No other form of execution was acceptable to them. This was a strategic move on their part. In the Jewish culture, the most despicable criminals were executed, and their bodies were hung on trees. Deuteronomy 21:23 says, "Anyone hanging on a tree is cursed of God." Death wasn't enough. The leaders wanted to use the shame of crucifixion as a means to further disgrace and discredit Christ.

Their tactic worked on some people. Even after the events of the Resurrection, some Jews wouldn't accept Christ as Messiah because they couldn't believe that the Messiah would be the kind of person who was crucified. And the shame of the cross was too much for some weak Christians who were too embarrassed to admit that they followed Jesus, who had been crucified. The apostle Paul commented on the shame of the cross, which prevented Jews from seeing Christ as the Messiah:

> *I know very well how foolish the message of the cross sounds to those who are on the road to destruction. But we who are being saved recognize this message as the very power of God....God's way seems foolish to the Jews because they want a sign*

*from heaven to prove it is true. And it is foolish to
the Greeks because they believe only what agrees
with their own wisdom. So when we preach that
Christ was crucified, the Jews are offended, and the
Gentiles say it's all nonsense* (1 Corinthians
1:18,22-23).

The cross can still symbolize shame and scandal, but
the meaning is slightly different in our contemporary
culture.

The cross symbolizes the fact that Christ's salvation is
not reserved for holy and perfect people (which none of
us happen to be). Christ went to the cross to save imperfect people, who are guilty of sin. If you feel ashamed of
things you have done in the past, you are exactly the
kind of person Christ was thinking of as He hung on the
cross.

The cross symbolizes the fact that the Christian life
includes its share of difficulties. Christianity isn't about
living in a stained-glass world where everything is nice,
clean, and easy. Christianity means hardship. Each
Christian has to carry a figurative cross. Jesus promised
this to the disciples in John 16:2.

Why Did Christ Have to Die?

If God makes up all the rules for life (and He does),
why didn't He just arrange things so that we could be
saved without requiring the death of Christ? That's a
good question, and the answer remains a bit of a mys-
tery. The Bible doesn't explain it all, but it tells us this
much:

Christ had to die *because of who God is*. Yes, God can
make up the rules, but He can't change His own nature.
The nature of God is perfect, and He can't tolerate sin.

He is a God of holiness and divine justice. Because of who God is, sin must be punished.

Christ had to die *because of who we are.* Humanity is totally depraved. That doesn't mean that there is no kindness within us at all. Most of us are mixtures of good and bad. But even the best of us is not totally good. Depravity describes the infection of sin throughout our entire being: our body, our mind, our emotions, our will, and our spirit. Total depravity means that we are completely unable to extract ourselves from our sinful condition. We are spiritually dead in our sins.

> *Once you were dead, doomed forever because of your many sins. You used to live just like the rest of the world, full of sin, obeying Satan....All of us used to live that way, following the passions and desires of our evil nature. We were born with an evil nature, and we were under God's anger just like everyone else* (Ephesians 2:1-3).

Christ had to die *because of who He is.* If God is holy and requires that sin be punished, and if we are sinful, we need help. That's where Christ came in, and that's why He had to die. He was the only perfect one who could be a sacrifice for our sins. Only Christ could die in our place so that we didn't have to suffer the penalty that we deserved.

> *For God made Christ, who never sinned, to be the offering for our sin, so that we could be made right with God through Christ* (2 Corinthians 5:21).

◼ ◻ ◻

Study the Word

1. About 700 years before the Crucifixion, the prophet Isaiah gave a description about the coming Messiah. This seemed to be a bizarre and confusing prophecy at the time it was made because it portrayed the Messiah as a victim rather than a victor. Read Isaiah 53:1-12 for this description. Identify the ways in which Christ's life matches Isaiah's portrayal.

2. Even before His Crucifixion, Jesus equated the Christian life with carrying the burden of a cross. Read Matthew 16:24. What did Jesus mean by "carrying your cross" if you want to follow Him?

3. Read Psalm 22:14-18,31; 69:3; Isaiah 50:6. In what ways does John's account of the events leading up to the Crucifixion match these Old Testament prophecies?

4. Describe how the disciples might have felt at the moment of Christ's Crucifixion.

5. Read Romans 6:23, Ephesians 1:7; 2:8-9; Colossians 1:19-22; Hebrews 2:14-17. What do these passages say about Christ's death and what it accomplished?

Chapter 12

The biggest fact about Joseph's tomb was
that it wasn't a tomb at all—it was a room
for a transient. Jesus just stopped there a
night or two on his way back to glory.

—Herbert Booth Smith

A Different Agenda

John's Gospel was the last of the four biographies of Christ to be written. John expected that his readers already knew about Christ's Crucifixion, burial, and Resurrection.

So John wasn't writing for merely informational purposes. He knew many of the facts were covered by the other Gospels, so he had a different agenda: to confront his readers with the authenticity of Jesus. Christ claimed to be God, and what John tells in the next two chapters is going to prove He was telling the truth.

RESURRECTION: Up, Out, and Walking Around

John 20

*T*hree days pass between the end of chapter 19 and the first verse of chapter 20. Mary, enshrouded in that Sunday morning's predawn stillness, came to pay her respects at the tomb of Christ, but she found it empty. This was the very first Easter, but nobody knew it yet.

No Ordinary Stone

At the time of Christ, rich people, such as Joseph of Arimathea, arranged for their burial well in advance of their death. The wealthy had above-ground tombs that were often caves in hillsides. A small ditch was dug at the entrance, and a huge boulder would be rolled in front of the entrance. Since the stone rested in the ditch, rolling the stone away once it was in place was almost impossible.

When Mary came to the grave early on Sunday morning, she saw that the stone had been moved away from the entrance. She reasonably assumed that the Jewish leaders or Roman authorities had taken Christ's body. After all, Roman soldiers had been posted at the tomb immediately following Christ's burial.

The stone in front of Christ's grave was just a plain old rock. But it has taken on great symbolism to all followers of Christ.

As we study that stone at Christ's tomb, we need to ask ourselves some questions:

- It is a *memorial stone*. This stone represents Christ's victory over death. It is a memorial to the fact that He is the Messiah. If He had been only a mortal, He'd still be in the grave, and the stone would still be in place. What type of stone will mark your grave when you die? Will it be just a tombstone that says you were once alive, but now you're dead? Or will it be a memorial stone that celebrates the fact that you passed from earthly life to eternal life?

- It is a *foundation stone*. The Resurrection of Christ is the cornerstone of our Christian faith. The Crucifixion would have been insufficient without the Resurrection. Any person could have died for us, but anyone else's death could never pay the penalty for our sins. Our salvation required the death of someone perfect and sinless. Only the

Son of God could perform this task, and Christ's Resurrection proved His credentials. Are you placing your hope of salvation on anything other than the cornerstone of Christ's death and Resurrection? Are you thinking that you'll get into heaven because you are basically a good person? Are you hoping that you've earned enough brownie points with God to avoid hell? Don't build your hopes on anything other than the firm foundation of Christ, who defeated death by His Resurrection.

• It is a *marker stone*. As a sign on a highway marks the boundary between counties, the stone at Christ's tomb marks the boundary between the living and the dead. Those who reject Christ stand on the side of spiritual death. On the other side of the stone are those who follow Him and worship Him. On which side of the stone are you?

The Meaning of the Empty Tomb

John was the "other disciple" (John 20:2-4) who ran to inspect the empty tomb with Peter. In John 20:8, John says that he "saw and believed," but he doesn't say what he saw or what he believed. From the context, we know that he saw an empty tomb. From the prior claims of Christ, we know what he believed—that Jesus was truly the Son of God.

The Resurrection proved certain things, not only to John and Peter, but to the world:

• It validated Christ's claim of Messiahship.

• It validated Christ's teaching.

- It validated Christ's predictions that He would conquer death.

- It proved Christ's supernatural nature.

- It proved that the religious leaders were wrong when they labeled Jesus a fraud.

Mary Can't Believe Her Eyes
(John 20:11-18)

Jesus made many personal appearances after His Resurrection. The first was to Mary Magdalene, who had come earlier to visit the tomb but then ran to get Peter and John. She had returned with them to the tomb not fully comprehending its significance. She was still grieving when Jesus approached her in the garden. Although she was one of Christ's closest friends, her grief prevented her from recognizing Him. She supposed Him to be the cemetery gardener.

Mary's experience is a lesson for all of us. We should never get so wrapped up in our grief that we don't recognize Christ. He is there for us in our time of sorrow. That's when He wants to comfort us. We should be expecting to see Him.

Behind Closed Doors (John 20:19-23)

Although they were excited that Jesus had risen from the dead, the disciples were gathered in a private room behind closed doors on that Sunday evening. The Jewish leaders and Roman authorities were already trying to cover up Christ's Resurrection by spreading a lie that the disciples had stolen Christ's body. Fearful of arrest, the disciples were keeping a low profile. They were undercover, but Christ found them anyway. With the doors still locked, He simply appeared in the middle of the room. What a reunion that must have been!

As any guest who shows up uninvited might do, Jesus brought a gift with Him. It was the gift of the Holy Spirit. In a fashion reminiscent of when God breathed life into Adam (see Genesis 2:7), Jesus breathed the Holy Spirit into the disciples. This fulfilled the promise of the Holy Spirit that Jesus had given to the disciples in the Upper Room. Energized with this new supernatural power, the disciples were equipped to spread the word of Christ's salvation. Of course, they needed a little instruction. When Christ explained that they could forgive anyone's sins (20:23), He wasn't implying that they had God's power of forgiveness. He was merely explaining that they had the privilege of presenting the Gospel message and confirming to new believers that their sins were forgiven by Christ's death on the cross.

You Can Touch This (John 20:24-29)

Not all of the 11 remaining disciples were present in that locked room. Thomas was missing, and he proved to be skeptical of what the others told him. In writing his Gospel, John never missed an opportunity to tell about someone's reaction when they were confronted with Jesus. We should not be surprised that John spent a few verses telling about Thomas' subsequent meeting with Christ. Jesus made another personal appearance before the disciples eight days later, and this time Thomas was there. When Jesus instructed Thomas to touch the nail holes in His hands, Thomas was convinced!

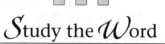

$\mathcal{S}$tudy the $\mathcal{W}$ord

1. As you read John 20:1-18, imagine the emotions Mary must have felt. Perhaps you can add to this list. How would recognizing Jesus affect each of these emotions?

   • confusion

   • despair

   • sorrow

   • anger

   Can you think of a time when "recognizing Jesus" in the middle of your difficult circumstances changed your entire perspective?

2. Jesus sent the disciples and empowered them for their mission (John 20:21-23). List some of the parallels between the Father sending Jesus and Jesus sending the disciples. Do you think the disciples understood what Jesus was saying?

3. What is your impression of Thomas (John 20:24-29)? What attitude does Jesus seem to have toward Thomas? In what ways have you been like Thomas in the past?

4. When do you think John and Peter realized Jesus was
    alive? Was it when Mary talked to them, as they were
    running to the tomb, or after they found the tomb
    empty? How about you? Describe the circumstance
    of the moment when you first realized who Christ is
    and what He has done for you.

5. Thomas had to see Christ to believe in Him. Obvi-
    ously, you can't see Jesus or touch Him as did
    Thomas. What brought you to the point of believing
    in Christ? What convinced you to put your faith in
    Him?

Chapter 13

The Gospel of John is an amazing book. It can be read and loved without any commentary at all. But the more we study John, the more wealth arises out of it.... There is many a phrase in John whose greatness will not be exhausted in a lifetime, let alone in a single day.

—*William Barclay*

The Anticlimax

Chapter 20 of John might have left you at a spiritual high point because it ended with one of the most dynamic verses in the entire Bible. But don't think that the Gospel of John ends with a bang. Apparently John had a few last details that needed some clarification.

Completion: Loose Ends and New Beginnings

John 21

*I*f you ask our opinion (which you haven't, but we'll offer it anyway), the book of John has a great ending with the last verse of chapter 20:

> *But these are written so that you may believe that Jesus is the Messiah, the Son of God, and that by believing in him you will have life* (John 20:31).

After the presentation of the Crucifixion and the Resurrection, and after reiterating the purpose of what he wrote, John is at a high point. What a great place to end.

But John didn't end his book there. He added one more chapter. It's a chapter that seems a bit strange because it's so anticlimactic. And that's the reason why it's worth studying. It must have some important meaning if John was compelled to include it.

The facts that John presents are rather straightforward:

- Jesus saw the disciples fishing on the Sea of Galilee, and they joined Him for breakfast on the shore.

- Jesus had a conversation about Peter's commitment to Him.

- Jesus talked to Peter briefly about his future.

- Jesus dismissed Peter's question about John.

That's all John wrote. Not much more, and certainly nothing earth-shattering. But, remember that John often has a meaning behind the story, and that's the case here.

He's Really Real (John 21:1-14)

Many people witnessed the Resurrection of Christ. His reappearance wasn't just limited to one or two individuals. Literally hundreds of people saw Him. This fact was never honestly disputed by the Jewish leaders. They knew that Jesus was resurrected, so they bribed the Roman soldiers who had been guarding the tomb to spread the rumor that the disciples had stolen Christ's body. (See Matthew 28:11-15.)

As time passed, however, opponents of Christianity began to discredit the eyewitness accounts of Christ's Resurrection. Here are some of the things they said:

- The disciples and the others were hallucinating when they thought they saw Jesus. He was never really there, except in their imaginations.

- What they saw wasn't really Jesus in a resurrected body, but rather some sort of ghost or spirit. They weren't looking at the genuine article; they saw something else and assumed it was Christ.

- Maybe the disciples saw Jesus, but He didn't have a real body as they said. He was just a spirit, so He didn't really rise from the dead. What the disciples saw was just the afterlife spirit of the dead Christ.

Imagine how offensive such accusations must have been to John and all of Christ's followers. Such arguments denied the very fact of the Resurrection and, thereby, denied Christ's claim to be the Son of God.

Through the very subtle story in John 21:1-14, John underscores the fact that Jesus was resurrected in bodily form by giving details such as these:

- Jesus had a charcoal fire going on the beach.

- Jesus had a fried fish meal waiting for the disciples.

- Jesus ate breakfast with the disciples.

This story is John's way of emphasizing that Jesus was resurrected in bodily form. This was no fire-making, fish-frying, breakfast-eating hallucination. This Jesus was the real deal.

---

*W*hat's the *S*ignificance of the 153 *F*ish?

John seems to make a big point about the 153 fish in the net (see John 21:11). Who cares? But if John mentioned it, he must have had a reason. We think some scholars have stretched a bit to find significance in the number 153.

One opinion is that there are 10 commandments, and 7 is considered the perfect number. 10 + 7 = 17, and 153 is the sum of all numbers from 1 through 17.

Another viewpoint is that 153 *varieties* of fish existed. The net represents the Christian church, and the story illustrates that the church is open to people from every nationality and race. (Nice try, but we think this only works if you assume that exactly 153 varieties of fish existed.)

We think this is just one of the questions that will remain unanswered until we get to heaven (where we probably won't care that much about it once we are in the presence of the Lord God Almighty). But you can feel free to ask God about it if the question is bugging you.

Three Times Asked, Three Times Answered (John 21:15-17)

Another vignette in this chapter finds Jesus asking Peter the same question three times: "Peter, do you love me?" At the first instance, Jesus presents the question this way: "Do you love me more than these?" What He meant by "these" is not clear. Three possibilities exist:

1. Jesus could have gestured with His arm to all of the surrounding items: the fishing boat, the nets, and the fish. In other words, He could have been asking if Peter loved Him more than his career. If asked this way, Jesus would want to know if Peter was willing to forsake his prior lifestyle and occupation for the difficult life of being a witness for Christ. (This would be a valid question since Peter had now come to realize that following Christ wasn't always easy.)

2. Jesus could have been referring to the other disciples who were present: "Do you love me more than you love James and John, Thomas and Nathanael?"

3. Perhaps Jesus was asking whether Peter considered his love for Christ to be greater than the love that the other disciples had for Him. If this was the question, then it would be, "Do you love me more than these other disciples love me?"

Peter's response was simply: "You know I love you." This humble response suggests that Peter understood the question in the third sense. While in the Upper Room, Peter had boasted a proclamation of love that was greater than the other disciples'. His denials of Christ in the courtyard had given him a new sense of reality. Now he was content to simply declare his love without comparison to others.

Wasn't Christ gracious to give Peter three opportunities to declare his love? He provided one for each time Peter had denied Christ.

Feed My Sheep

In each response to Peter's declaration of love, Christ tells Peter to care for His sheep. This is a clear reference to Peter's role in what would be the fledgling Christian church. Christ wanted Peter to care for the new Christians as a shepherd would care for his flock of sheep. This would require Peter to lead, feed, and protect the new Christians.

Notice how Jesus makes a connection between loving Him and caring for others. Christ seemed to be saying, "Peter, if you love Me, show it by loving others." *Saying* that we love Christ is relatively easy. But we prove it when we extend our love to others. Does this remind you of Christ's Upper Room discussion of the importance of love? (See John 13:15,35; 15:12.) Have you been showing your love for Christ by loving others?

Your Death Will Be like This (John 21:18-19)

John 21:19 says that Jesus let Peter know what kind of death he would suffer by the things Jesus said in verse 18. Read verse 18 and see if you can find a clue. It actually contains three clues:

- stretch out your hands

- others will direct you

- where you don't want to go

While the meaning may be disguised to us, it wasn't to Peter. Christ was referring to the fact that Peter would be killed by crucifixion. (Get it? With his arms stretched out on a cross.) Peter was crucified in Rome under the reign of Nero around A.D. 65. Tradition says that Peter asked to be hung upside down because he wasn't worthy to be crucified in the same manner as Christ.

Immediately after announcing that Peter would die in this gruesome manner, Jesus told him, "Follow me." This brings us back to another one of the Upper Room themes. Following Christ will not be easy. Persecution and suffering will be involved. (See John 16:1-4.) Are you prepared to endure hardship as you walk with Christ? Is your love for Him so strong that you would be willing to die for Him?

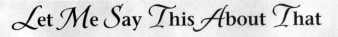

(John 21:20-23)

Scholars have wondered about the anticlimactic references to John in verses 20-23. Here again, John doesn't mention his own name directly, but the inference is clear. John wanted to clarify one point. Apparently a rumor persisted that John wasn't going to die and would live to see the return of Christ. In 21:23, John clarified the context of what Jesus said to dispel the rumor.

And in Conclusion (John 21:24-25)

Some scholars believe that John had a personal reason for concluding his Gospel with the discussion about Peter. Some people in the first-century Christian church might have been placing John on a pedestal and denigrating Peter's role. After all, John was "the disciple whom Jesus loved," and Peter was the disciple who denied Christ. In this last chapter of his Gospel, John intends to show that Jesus had forgiven Peter and that Jesus had specifically charged Peter with an instrumental role in the early church.

And what about John's role? It is described in the last two verses of chapter 21. John's role is to be a witness and present a fresh and intimate portrait of who Christ is, what He did, and what He taught.

Throughout his Gospel, John has presented an amazing "behind the scenes" view of Christ. He concludes by saying that a full description of Christ couldn't be contained in all of the books in the world (John 21:25). That statement begs the question that is artfully woven through John: How do you respond to this person of Jesus Christ? This is the question for those who came face-to-face with Jesus: the disciples, Nicodemus, the Chief Priests and Pharisees, the Samaritan woman, the lame man, Pilate, and others. After their respective encounters with Jesus, they were never the same. Their lives had been irrevocably changed. And now, through your study of John, you too have come face-to-face with Jesus. Your life cannot be the same now that you have met Him so personally. So, how do you respond? Do you consider Him to be the Son of God? Are you choosing to follow Him, knowing that service and sacrifice are proof that your love is genuine?

■ ■ ■

$\mathcal{S}$tudy the $\mathcal{W}$ord

1. List three or four different motivations Peter could have had for going fishing. What emotions might he have been experiencing?

2. Now make a second list: For each of the possible scenarios, what might Peter have felt when "they caught nothing all night"?

3. In John 21:15-23, what does Jesus' attitude toward Peter seem to be? Why do you think Jesus had this little after-breakfast chat with Peter?

4. Now that you have come face-to-face with Jesus through your study of John, what response might Jesus be inviting you to make? In other words, at this stage of your Christian pilgrimage, how will you respond to Jesus' invitation, "Follow me"?

5. All the way through the Gospel of John, you have seen the response of people who came face-to-face with Jesus. How has your study of the Gospel of John affected you spiritually? How has your encounter with Jesus in the Gospel of John changed you?

Dig Deeper

$\mathcal{W}$e are self-proclaimed nonexperts. But don't worry; we do our homework before we write a book. We do extensive study and background research and read those thick books with tiny print. If you want to check out our resources, here they are (and we hope that you'll be so interested in the Gospel of John that you'll want to read a few of them for yourself):

Commentaries

You may have to look hard to find a copy, but *John: The Gospel of Belief* by Merrill C. Tenney is excellent. Professor Tenney was the Dean of the Graduate School at Wheaton College.

A more recent entry in the commentary category is the *John* volume of the Life Application Bible Commentary series. The language, examples, and applications are very current.

One of the classic traditional commentary series on the New Testament was written by William Barclay. He's got that rare combination of being both insightful and understandable. There is a two-volume set on John from his Daily Study Bible Series.

Some people feel that the best commentary on the Gospel of John is written by Leon Morris. His commentary is interesting, but his title is rather bland: *Commentary on the Gospel of John*.

Sometimes the commentaries we used weren't just on John but covered the entire New Testament. That is the case with The New Testament volume of *The Bible Knowledge Commentary*, edited by John Walvoord and Roy Zuck.

Likewise, there is a single volume covering the entire New Testament for the *IVP Bible Background Commentary* by Craig S. Keener. This is the book to use if you are particularly interested in the cultural customs.

We have in our libraries two other single-volume commentaries on the whole Bible that are well-worn: *Matthew Henry's Commentary* and *The Wycliffe Bible Commentary*.

General Bible Study Helps

Modesty prohibits us from suggesting our own *Bruce & Stan's Guide to the Bible*. We can't even force ourselves to mention *Bruce & Stan's Pocket Guide to Studying Your Bible*. These are great "user-friendly" resources, but you didn't hear that from us.

We hope you are experiencing the rewards of studying the Bible. If you are ready to be a real student of the Word, then you might want to read *How to Study Your Bible* by Kay Arthur. Get your colored pencils ready because you'll be using them if you follow Kay's disciplined approach.

Speaking of being a student, sometimes a "survey" course is helpful for a general overview. We like the textbook written by Robert H. Gundry, *A Survey of the New Testament*. This book can give you an overall perspective. It devotes a separate chapter to the Gospel of John.

Bible Translations

We intend that you read the Bible right along with this book. It is more important that you actually read the Gospel of John than a book about John.

There are many translations of the Bible available to you. We suggest that your primary study Bible be a *literal* translation (as opposed to a paraphrase), such as the *New International Version* (NIV) of the Bible or the *New American Standard Bible* (NASB). However, it's perfectly acceptable to use a Bible paraphrase, such as *The Living Bible* or *The Message* in your devotional reading.

In this book we have been using the *New Living Translation* (NLT), a Bible translation that uses a method called "dynamic equivalence." This means that the scholars who translated the Bible from the original languages (Hebrew and Greek) used a "thought for thought" translation philosophy rather than a "word for word" approach. It's just as accurate but easier to read. In the final analysis, the Bible that's best for you is the Bible you enjoy reading because you can understand it.

A word about personal pronouns: Did you notice that we prefer to capitalize all personal pronouns that refer to God, Jesus, and the Holy Spirit (such as *He, Him,* and *His*)? Some writers don't; we do. It's just a matter of personal preference. In fact, personal pronouns for God were not capitalized in the original languages, which is why you'll find that the Bible uses *he, him, his,* and *himself.* We do it in symbolic reverence and to remind ourselves how big God is and how small we are.

The authors of this book would enjoy hearing from you. Contact them with your questions, comments, or to schedule them to speak at an event.

Twelve Two Media Group
PO Box 25997
Fresno, CA 93729-5997

E-mail: info@TwelveTwoMedia.com

Web site: www.TwelveTwoMedia.com

Christianity 101™ Bible Studies

Genesis: Discovering God's Answers to Life's Ultimate Questions
What did God have in mind when He started this world? What happened to His perfect design? As readers join Bruce & Stan in this exciting survey, they will learn how God's record of ancient times impacts *our* time.

Ephesians: Finding Your Identity in Christ
This inviting little guide to the book of Ephesians gets straight to the heart of Paul's teaching on the believer's identity in Christ: We belong to Christ, the Holy Spirit is our guarantee, and we can share in God's power.

John: Encountering Christ in a Life-Changing Way
John records how Jesus changed the lives of everyone He met. Bruce and Stan's fresh approach to these narratives will help readers have their own personal, life-changing encounters with Jesus, the Son of God.

Revelation: Unlocking the Mysteries of the End Times
Just what is really going to happen? In this fascinating look at the apostle John's prophecy, Bruce & Stan demonstrate why—when God's involved—the end of the world is something to look forward to.

Exclusive Online Feature

Here's a Bible study feature you're really going to like!
Simply go online at:

www.christianity101online.com

There you'll find a Web site designed exclusively for users of the Christianity 101™ Bible Studies series. Just click on the book you are studying, and you will discover additional information, resources, and helps, including...

- *Background Material*—We can't put everything in this Bible study, so this online section includes more material, such as historical, geographical, theological, and biographical information.

- *More Questions*—Do you need more questions for your Bible study? Here are additional questions for each chapter. Bible study leaders will find this especially helpful.

- *Answers to Your Questions*—Do you have a question about something in your Bible study? Post your question and an "online scholar" will respond.

- *FAQs*—In this section are answers to some of the more frequently asked questions about the book you are studying.

What are you waiting for? Go online and become a part of the Christianity 101™ community!

Bruce & Stan's® *Guide Series:*

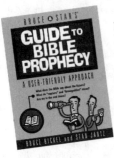

Bruce & Stan's® Guide to Bible Prophecy
Dealing with prophecy and end times in their witty, down-to-earth way, Bruce and Stan offer the Bible's answers to readers' big questions. Is the end really near? Who is the Antichrist? What is the Rapture?

Bruce & Stan's® Guide to Cults, Religions, and Spiritual Beliefs
"Here is our purpose, plain and simple: to provide an understandable overview of predominant religions and spiritual beliefs (with a little sense of humor thrown in along the way)." Clear explanations help readers understand the core issues of more than a dozen religions.

Bruce & Stan's® Guide to God
This fresh, user-friendly guide to the Christian life is designed to help new believers get started or recharge the batteries of believers of any age. Humorous subtitles, memorable icons, and learning aids present even difficult concepts in a simple way. Perfect for personal use or group study.

Knowing the Bible 101
A fresh approach to making Christianity understandable—even the hard parts! This user-friendly book relies on humor, insights, and relevant examples that will inspire readers not only to make sense of Scripture, but to *enjoy* Bible study.